After the Merger:
Managing the Shockwaves

After the Merger: Managing the Shockwaves

Price Pritchett
Pritchett and Associates, Inc.
Dallas, Texas

International rights and foreign translations available only through negotiation with
Pritchett & Associates, Inc.
ISBN 0-944002-20-X

Library of Congress Catalog Card No. 84-73046

Printed in the United States of America

To Patty, Kim, Julie, and P.J.

Preface

This is a book about the human side of mergers and acquisitions. It is written for the executive who is involved in acquiring firms and for the businessman whose company is being acquired and merged.

Many people have written at length about how to structure a merger/acquisition, about how to handle the legal and financial aspects of deal making. But there has not been one single book that focuses on the tasks and problems of postmerger management. This is rather amazing, given the fact that practically everyone agrees that people issues and postmerger problems are what cause most deals to go sour.

But there are signs that the business world is finally beginning to recognize the corporate trauma caused by mergers. *Fortune* magazine estimates that 25 to 50 percent of the work force is directly affected when two companies merge. And it is calculated that almost a quarter of a million employees' lives were changed as a result of the 10 largest mergers that occurred in 1983.

The hard dollars an acquirer forks over to buy another firm usually don't represent the full price tag. The people problems and managerial difficulties that subsequently develop are also a very important factor, and we might refer to the tangible and intangible costs they generate as the hidden economics of the deal.

This book begins by taking an honest, hard look at the statistics on merger success. The numbers are pretty gloomy—quite a bit like the statistics on marriage and divorce in the United States (while getting married is relatively easy and almost always exciting, being married can be painful and very difficult).

The second chapter provides an organized way of looking at different merger/acquisition climates. The varying circumstances that give rise to an acquisition breed quite discrepant management problems, but the book goes on to highlight the broad similarities virtually all mergers share. These psychological shockwaves are explained, giving the reader a good handle on what to expect—such that the problems can be attacked in a more informed fashion.

Three chapters are devoted to the issue of staffing decisions that must be made. A solid argument is offered for careful management succession planning that grows out of a rich, objective database. Then the book turns its attention to how a merger generates a strong swell of "organizational dissonance," a new phenomenon that is almost certain to be either a strong force for good or a highly destructive influence in a company. Guidelines are offered on how to make a merger a "recharging event" for a firm. Finally, the last chapters give a managers' checklist on concrete actions that should be taken by the management teams in both the parent company and the target firm.

Until now, managers and executives who have had the job of making a merger successful have had to really scrounge around looking for the kind of help and information provided in this book. If they were lucky, they may have stumbled onto an occasional article about the people dynamics of mergers. But the odds were against them. Even if they did find something to read on the topic now and then, they likely finish it feeling that something was missing—such as specific answers, clear-cut coaching, and state-of-the-art thinking on how to maximize a merger's people potential. Even the best workshops and seminars in the country have historically short-changed this aspect of mergers and acquisitions.

In over a decade of consulting—to billion dollar outfits and small privately held companies—my firm has frequently been called in to help unravel organizational tangles caused by mergers and acquisitions. Again and again we have seen top executives trying to sort out problems that could have been easily prevented—or at least greatly minimized. This book represents an attempt to share our experience in a way that can be immediately put to use by today's businessmen.

Price Pritchett

Acknowledgments

I wish to express special thanks to Dr. Jerry Roemisch for his conceptual help in the preparation of this manuscript, particularly in Chapters 2 and 3. Appreciation is also due Dr. Ron Pound of our staff, who willingly picked up the slack in our consulting work while I was absorbed in writing this book. Sincere thanks also go to Diana Nestler and Joyce Ferguson for being so patient and helpful in typing the manuscript and keeping a sharp eye out for improvements that could be made.

Finally, I would like to express appreciation to *Forbes* and *Fortune* magazines for permission to use quotes from their publications, and Peter Drucker for permission to quote from an article of his in *The Wall Street Journal*.

P. P.

Contents

Introduction

Mergers and acquisitions serve as one form of corporate growth, and it's worth remembering that growth, whether in an individual or an organization, frequently brings with it some discomfort as well as some awkward behavior. How can executives and managers best handle these growing pains? What can be done to overcome the adolescent clumsiness that comes from newly developed corporate muscle not yet matched by coordination?

The best steps probably are preventive ones. But because of the nature of acquisitions—how the deals are pursued, negotiated, and finally struck—many problems cannot be preempted. They can only be anticipated, met head-on, and dealt with in a professional and timely manner.

Certainly one of the things top management can do is be prepared for the organizational dissonance that is virtually always one of the upshots of merger/acquisition activity. The destabilizing force that is generated opens the door for change, for positive effect. It is a motivating force top management can seize to fuel growth and improve performance. It is energy that can be harnessed.

Indeed, the dissonance must be managed intelligently and carefully channeled or it can be disastrous. It is not something to be stifled, sidestepped, or ignored. It should be parlayed into a positive thrust, but only rarely is it exploited as it should be for its potential benefit to both of the firms involved.

Often the dissonance, the psychological shockwaves, appear to be unexpected, poorly understood, and inadequately governed. As a result, there is much organizational trauma that could have been avoided, and many potential benefits of the dissonance are not seized. The people responsible for engineering mergers and acquisitions have exhibited a high degree of expertise in handling the legal and financial aspects of the deal. In fact, during the past several years, the sophistication of both takeover attempts and merger defenses has grown rapidly. Regrettably, there has not been a corresponding increase in the sophistication of postmerger management. And regardless of how astute a job the negotiators do, the merger is not going be a bargain if management doesn't make it work.

So this is a book about managing, rather than making, mergers and acquisitions. The intent is to sharpen managerial insight and understanding into the unique dynamics that characterize this form of corporate development. It is an effort to give direction and straightforward answers to executives and managers who must carry the burden of making the merger measure up to the potential that was originally conceived by the deal makers.

Every year there are thousands of acquisitions that must be shepherded by new owners and managers, and these people need guidelines, plus a frame of reference that makes sense out of the people problems that are peculiar to this sort of organizational event.

The symptomatology and underlying problems are remarkably consistent regardless of the size of the companies being acquired. It may be a mega deal such as DuPont buying Conoco, Sears acquiring Dean Witter, or Texaco attempting a takeover of Getty. It may be a big acquirer such as Alexander & Alexander making many small acquisitions of little independent insurance agencies, or a Dart and Kraft buy out of the small Churny company. There are innumerable owner/entrepreneurs who take their life savings and commit to a scary load of personal debt to buy some little business that another individual started but now wants to sell. Finally, there is a rapidly growing number of leveraged buyouts resulting from the trend toward divestiture or deconglomerating.

Granted, every single merger agreement that is reached will be unique in some respects, but there will be a remarkable number of features they all hold in common—enough that managers and executives can be told what to expect and how to contend with the situation most effectively.

That is the purpose of this book.

1

Problems in Buying a "Used" Company

It is lunchtime on a Thursday at the University Club in downtown Chicago. The three businessmen seated off by themselves at a table near the window are on their last cup of coffee. One is the CEO of an acquisition-minded pharmaceutical company. Another is the president of a major insurance company that recently bought a financial service firm. The third owns a small manufacturing company, and he is in the process of selling his firm. The lunch crowd is thinning out, but at this table the conversation isn't lagging.

The pharmaceutical executive leans to the table, eyes the other two, and growls, "It's a helluva lot like buying a second–hand car. We try to do our homework, but the preacquisition analyses never tell us all we need to know about how the outfit has been run. It's like kicking the tires, looking under the hood, and driving the car around the block. You're probably going to have a tough time seeing things the seller doesn't want you to see. Negotiations are the same whether you're buying a car or a company. That other guy is going to highlight the positives while concealing or downplaying problems. Every company we have bought since I became CEO has given us some nasty surprises."

Nodding and looking out the window across the Chicago skyline, the insurance company president adds, "We're facing the same problems right now with a company we just acquired. We're beginning to realize that the previous owner drove the car differently. When he owned the company it was one-man rule. But we operate in a decentralized fashion, so it's like the whole family has to know how to drive. The previous owner also pampered the machine, while our management style and philosophy is to drive hard. We're beginning to wonder if the acquisition will be able to handle the strain. On top of these problems, we have to deal with the negative press coverage we've been getting from the business journals. They keep writing that we're not knowledgeable about how to operate this kind of vehicle, that we don't have anybody who knows how to drive it. Where we really ran into problems was when we lost some of the seasoned executives we had expected would stay at the wheel, guys that had an outstanding track record."

The owner of the manufacturing firm grinned at his two companions and said, "So I'm supposed to have something in common with the used car salesman. Well, let me play with that for a minute. Sure,

I'm selling an organization that needs some repairs. I doubt that the people who are buying me out really know how well my company has been maintained. Furthermore, I don't know if they are mentally or financially prepared to make the repairs or, in other words, to give the organization what it needs."

"They plan on doing a minor tune-up, while you're sitting here knowing it really is due for a major overhaul, right?"

The owner/entrepreneur squinted back at the insurance company president and replied, "That's probably being a little too hard on me. Besides, I get the feeling that they're planning on dismantling the car and selling off some of the parts anyhow."

The CEO reflected on this for a few moments, then asked, "What happens to the whole when they sell off some of the parts? Is there going to be a breakdown? We tried that approach two years ago, and I guess we must have inadvertently sold the wheels, because that acquisition never went anywhere."

"Well, it's basically out of my hands," said the manufacturing executive. "There's a lot I could have told the guys who are buying me out, but they never asked the right questions. In fact, they haven't paid much attention to what I did tell them. The word I get from my old employees who are still with the company is that nobody's listening to them either. So what the hell? God helps those who help themselves."

As the three men got up from the table to leave, the president of the insurance company remarked, "I guess so. But whoever that guy was who said 'What you don't know can't hurt you' obviously didn't know beans about mergers and acquisitions."

STATISTICS ON MERGER SUCCESS AND FAILURE

Nobody has a very precise set of statistics regarding the success rate for mergers and acquisitions in the United States. One key reason is that, according to the Federal Trade Commission (FTC), approximately 60 percent of all merger activity is never publicized or consists of small transactions (less than million–dollar deals) that no one tracks systematically. According to the studies that have been conducted and the merger monitoring that is reported, though, growth through acquisition is a risky business.

Available statistics generally indicate that, on the whole, acquirers have less than a 50-50 chance of being successful in merger/acquisition ventures.

Granted, *success* is a qualitative issue. Also, what looks like success today may subsequently turn out to be a fiasco, while current disappointment can sometimes blossom forth and become an outstanding money-maker. But the grim facts remain—far too many mergers go bad.

A study by Acquisition Horizons involving data on 537 companies that had made at least one acquisition within a five-year time frame produced discouraging statistics. Over 40 percent of the respondents described their acquisition efforts as only *somewhat successful* or *unsuccessful*. The most frequently mentioned reason for the disappointing results was that management in the acquired firm was not as deep as expected. Other major reasons were that the preacquisition research proved inadequate or inaccurate, the systems were not as well developed as had been thought, a new strategic plan was needed for the acquired firm, integration planning was not all that it should have been, and, finally, some of the key management talent left the firm. The companies studied ranged in size from $125 million to over $2 billion in annual sales.

Another recent study conducted by *Fortune* magazine analyzed 10 major conglomerate acquisitions made during 1971.[1] All acquisitions represented a move by the parent company into a new line of business, and the question posed by the study was "Do conglomerate mergers make sense?" Figure 1-1, pp. 10-11 charts the key data from the *Fortune* study and offers the answer that, at least at the end of the 10-year period when this backward look occurred, they did not.

The most favorable results, based on a calculation that allowed comparisons on the basis of earnings per share, showed half of the acquisitions to have positive numbers (Squibb Corporation, RCA, ITT, American Cyanamid Company, and Johns-Manville Corporation) while the other five (Heublein, Inc., Schering Corporation, Nabisco

---

[1]Arthur M. Louis, 'The Bottom Line on 10 Big Mergers," *Fortune* 105 (May 3, 1982)

Brands, Inc., Northwest Industries, Inc., and General Host Corporation) showed negative results. Not one of the ten acquisitions measured up to the *Fortune* 500 median return-on-investment statistic of 13.8 percent for the same period. Only two mergers out of the ten (ITT-Scott and Johns-Manville-Holophane) made it through the 10-year period of the study without experiencing significant difficulties. A final statistic highlighted by the *Fortune* study concerned the investment potential of the acquiring companies during the period from 1971 through 1981. Five of them—Heublein, RCA, ITT, Schering Plough and Johns-Manville (since renamed Manville Corporation) ended up reflecting a negative return. Northwest is the only firm studied that ranked in *Fortune* 500's top 50 companies in total return to investors for the 10-year period ending with 1981. It ranked 38th, while none of the other 9 firms managed to rank anywhere in the upper half of the top 500.

The obvious question is "What's going wrong?" Undoubtedly all acquirers are well-intentioned in their growth plans and fully expect to be successful in the buying and blending of other firms. Some of the failures and disappointments can be legitimately explained away, attributed to something like an unfavorable economic turn of events. Sometimes the acquisition was a mismatch in the first place, with small odds for success. A high percentage of merger difficulties and failures, though, derives directly from faulty management. Target companies are strategically sought and strategically stalked, but then the follow-up acts are poorly orchestrated. People issues are mishandled as the acquirer improvises instead of following a strategically designed, systematically conducted program for corporate integration.

MERGER/ACQUISITION MANAGEMENT CHALLENGES

Moving into New Territory

Some acquisitions are inherently much more risky than others.

Figure 1-1 The 10 biggest conglomerate acquisitions made by 1971's *Fortune 500*

Acquiring company/ Acquired company	Price	% of book value	Industry	Acquirer's 1981 profits/ Acquisition's share (estimated)	1981 earnings per share of acquirer		What the acquirer said about the acquisition	
					Actual	Hypothetical (if acquisition hadn't been made)	*Then*	*Recently*
Schering/ Plough	$644 million in common and preferred stock	815	Drugs Cosmetics, Toiletries	$179 million/ $44 million	$3.31	$4.08	The two companies complement each other well. Schering's research and international operations will benefit Plough.	Schering's international people didn't adapt well to consumer products. That synergism took longer than we thought.
Heublein/ Kentucky Fried Chicken	$237 million in common stock	427	Alcoholic beverages Fast food outlets	$88 million/ $22 million	$4.09	$4.11	Gives us a strong position in fast foods; provides immediate new dimensions and promising prospects.	We learned the hard way; we made our share of mistakes, we took too long to move down the learning curve.
Squibb/ Lanvin-Charles of the Ritz	$206 million in common stock	426	Drugs Cosmetics, Fragrances	$105 million/ $15 million	$2.10	$2.01	The proxy statement can't spell out the growth opportunities that we believe lie ahead of Lanvin-Charles of the Ritz.	We made some mistakes because we didn't understand the business. But our direction was correct.
RCA/ Coronet Industries	$187 million in common stock	515	Electronics Carpet	$54 million/ $5 million	($.19)	($.28)	Should provide valuable diversification in an important consumer growth area.	We will consider the sale of Coronet when market conditions warrant.
Northwest Industries/ Buckingham	$120 million in cash and notes	736	Conglomerate Alcoholic beverages	$419 million/ $4 million	$14.20	Not calculable	Buckingham is a fine company with a strong earnings record.	Of importance in 1991 was the unsolicited cash sale of our beverages segment; sale was a proper strategic move.

Company	Price		Business	Sales / Income	EPS before	EPS after	Comments
ITT/ O.M. Scott & Sons	$108 million in common stock	420	Conglomerate Lawncare products	$677 million $13 million	$4.58	$4.54	(ITT, perhaps because it was under antitrust attack in 1971, did not even issue a press release when Scott was acquired.) O.M. Scott is a leader in lawn care and gardening; its strength is evident in its higher revenue.
American Cyanamid/ Shulton	$106 million in common stock	169	Chemicals, drugs Toiletries, cosmetics	$197 million $14 million	$4.11	$4.08	Brought us a fine name with an excellent product line. We'd be a much more cyclical company if we didn't have Shulton. Synergy in research took too long to come.
General Host/ Cudahy	$80 million in cash	141	Food, retail stores Meatpacking	$14 million Not meaningful	$2.95	Not calculable	Represents a significant step toward our goal of acquiring businesses with proven earnings. The divestiture of Cudahy's meat business will minimize our vulnerability to this cyclical, commodity-driven business.
Nabisco[2]/ J.B. Williams	$72 million in common stock	Not available	Food Toiletries	$226 million $2 million	$4.21	$4.36	Represents planned expansion into consumer goods. (Nabisco would not talk to FORTUNE about J.B. Williams; several Wall Street analysts say Williams may soon be put up for sale.)
Johns-Manville[3]/ Holophane	$62 million in common stock	324	Building products Lighting fixtures	$60 million $8 million	$1.53	$1.27	Establishes John-Manville as a prominent entity in the field of lighting fixtures and components. During much of the past decade Holophane has distinguished itself as a contributor to our sales and earnings.

1 Now called Schering Plough.
2 Now called Nabisco Brands.
3 Now called Manville.
Source: Arthur M. Louis, "The Bottom Line On Big Mergers," *Fortune* (May 3, 1982), pp. 84-85.

The more difficult ones ordinarily represent a move in new directions by the acquirer and, since they are more troublesome, the parent firm should be prepared to invest more time, energy, and money in the integration effort. A strategic game plan is essential, one that is structured to deal with the predictable problems of the transition period yet allows the flexibility needed to accommodate contingency plans that invariably are called for.

Acquisition forays into a different industry or new line of business, for example, should be preceded by integration planning that respects the critical need to hang on to incumbents for the business savvy they possess. One management retention study has found that only one chief executive in ten still occupied his top management job two years after his company was acquired. Peter Drucker made the following comment about this risk factor in mergers/acquisitions:

> Within a year or so, the acquiring company must be able to provide top management for the company it acquired. It is an elementary fallacy to believe one can "buy" management. The buyer has to be prepared to lose the top incumbents in companies that are bought. Top people are used to being bosses; they don't want to be "division managers." If they were owners or part owners, the merger has made them so wealthy they don't have to stay if they don't enjoy it. And if they are professional managers without an ownership stake, they usually find another job easily enough.

Drucker then goes on to say that, "To recruit new top managers is a gamble that rarely comes off."[2]

Often people in *both* firms will be seriously troubled about how the acquisition may affect their personal careers, and part of the merger/acquisition planning should be aimed toward how these concerns will be addressed. By no means do people in the target company have a monopoly on this career uneasiness. When the Manor Care, Inc. chain of nursing homes acquired Quality Inns, Inc. (hotels/motels), one Manor Care senior executive lamented about how his organization had "blown its financial war chest" on an acquisition that had no relevance for his career growth. Meanwhile Quality Inn personnel experienced just as much dismay, and both firms suffered a loss of key talent.

---

[2] Peter F. Drucker, "The Five Rules of Successful Acquisition," *The Wall Street Journal*, October 15, 1981, p. 28.

Sometimes the lack of a strategically orchestrated and carefully monitored integration effort causes an impending merger to fall apart even before the final papers have been signed. A well-regarded international consulting firm of medium size reached agreement with one of the Big Eight accounting firms to merge forces. Even at the outset, though, the prospect of being acquired created serious apprehension throughout the smaller organization. Things got totally out of hand when representatives of the acquirer showed up to do merger data gathering at various regional offices of the consulting firm. People at these sites got the impression that they were being audited, and the resulting animosity was rapidly becoming unmanageable. That merger was subsequently called off, but follow-up efforts by the consulting firm to merge with another suitor were complicated by the "merger hangover" resulting from the first episode. The second potential acquirer was itself a subsidiary of a much larger parent company in still another business, and personnel in the consulting firm still gun-shy about how they were blitzed by the "auditors" were very leery of attempting any other linkups.

Culture Shock

Even when mergers and acquisitions involve two companies in the same industry, there can be dramatic cultural differences. Unless these are recognized, understood, and dealt with astutely in the integration efforts, the risk of failure increases significantly. Corporate culture may be a rather amorphous concept, but its influence is pervasive. Organizations that appear to be highly compatible and that seemingly should be able to achieve valuable merger synergies can have underlying cultures that seriously threaten coexistence.

Corporate culture is a peculiar blend of an organization's values, traditions, beliefs, and priorities. It is a sociological dimension that shapes management style as well as operating philosophies and practices. It helps determine what sort of behavior is rewarded in an organization, whether the rewards are tangible (salary, bonuses, promotions, perquisites, etc.) or intangible (respect, access to information, power, and so on). An organization's culture helps establish the norms and unwritten rules that guide employee actions. It legitimizes certain behavior and attitudes while disaffirming others.

In merger scenarios where markedly different cultures collide, employees find that behavior once sanctioned is no longer rewarded, maybe not even approved of, and perhaps even punished. The measuring stick invariably changes and, of course, new people are involved in taking the measurements. Incumbents are put on the defensive as they anticipate a threat to their corporate values and organizational lifestyle. As priorities blur and inconsistencies appear between new approaches and the old way of doing business, culture shock sets in. People first become confused, then frustrated, then resistant to change.

The conventional viewpoint is that Pan American World Airways, Inc.'s downhill slide was precipitated and complicated by its acquisition of National Airlines, Inc., a company with a very different culture. Efforts to blend the workforces met with incredible resistance and bred severe morale problems. Productivity and profitability declined steadily as negative employee attitudes were reflected in weaker job performance and customer-relations problems.

The potential for these problems is compounded when the merger involves international partners. American Express Company's acquisition of the privately held Trade Development Bank of Switzerland provides a good example of stylistic differences. The bank's culture is clubby, Old-World, and modulated. American Express is aggressive, hard driving, and numbers-oriented, with noticeably more willingness to take risks.

Some acquirers circumvent problems related to cultural differences by permitting their acquisitions to remain as free-standing operations with only minimal influence or involvement of the parent company. In many situations, however, it simply is not feasible to pursue that approach. For example, the economies of scale that could be accomplished by a merging of the two organizations may justify the efforts associated with reconciling the cultural differences that exist. But in those circumstances, a part of the integration strategy should be designing and scheduling a formally conducted compatibility study to gather data that will give shape to subsequent action plans.

When the huge Tenneco, Inc. conglomerate acquired Houston Oil and Minerals Corporation it made the time-worn pledge to keep the companies separate. But the promise turned out to be an empty one on two different counts. First, Houston Oil and Minerals personnel found that being governed by one of the country's biggest conglomerates meant they had to contend with a highly structured, bureaucratic parent firm that operated through a strict chain of command. The emphasis on budgeting and forecasting created massive amounts of paperwork. Incumbents complained about the system being impersonal as well as extremely frustrating, and Tenneco's insistence on a more cautious exploration program added to people's ire. Houston Oil and Minerals had a casual, freewheeling culture that nurtured aggressiveness and rewarded entrepreneurial spirit. The dramatic differences in corporate personality and organization structure caused people to leave in droves. Tenneco reportedly made a respectable effort to hang on to Houston Oil and Minerals employees, but in the end felt compelled to renege on its earlier commitment. A company memo explained that because of the loss of 34 percent of Houston Oil and Minerals management, 25 percent of its exploration staff, and 19 percent of its production people, it was impossible for the acquisition to remain a distinct unit.

Perhaps Tenneco could have done a better job of planning its postacquisition strategy. At the least, it should have showed greater respect for the way the merger integration activities intruded on the corporate culture of this target firm. One of the most common merger problems that can be found—and one that is apparent here—is the "violation of expectations" that alienates people in the acquisition. An acquirer raises false hope by assuring incumbents that nothing will change and that they will be allowed to conduct business as usual. Then the cultural conflicts begin to surface, antagonism toward the parent company mounts, and the risk of merger failure increases.

Variations in Operating Style

Companies can experience a very difficult postacquisition adjustment process simply as a result of having different operating styles.

Cultural variations per se may not be pronounced. But, for example, if one organization is highly decentralized and the other is accustomed to strong centralized control, there will be problems to work through. Operating strategies and practices of the two parties to the merger/acquisition can vary in a variety of other ways, too. Naturally, the more discrepancies that exist and the more pronounced these are, the greater the risk of failure. Integration strategies should be planned with the following thoughts in mind:

1. People, quite possibly in both companies, will be threatened and frustrated; these emotions will require attention.
2. Teaching and training will be necessary if the acquired firm's modus operandi is to be restructured such that it conforms with parent company practices.
3. Employees need to be given a good rationale for making the operating changes.
4. Top management should analyze whether there really is a need to reconcile the two different approaches, and this requires systematic data gathering and deliberation.
5. Top management should be patient and supportive during the transition period as people adapt to the required changes.

Employees in a company that has been led by a single dominant figure, perhaps an owner/entrepreneur, frequently feel lost when the company is acquired by a large, impersonal, and highly diversified conglomerate. Likewise, a loosely managed, highly individualistic firm has a wrenching adjustment process once it weds into a bureaucratic and highly structured organization.

Westinghouse Electric Corporation, an active acquirer, submits that it has been overwhelmingly unsuccessful in its efforts to retain the entrepreneurial owner/manager of the small and medium-sized business. A company paper states,

> The reason is not difficult to see. At the same time that we provide such a man with independent, moderate to substantial wealth, we impose upon him seemingly onerous constraints on his freedom to run "his" business as he had previously done. Overcoming having given that person both the motive and the means to leave you requires strong action if it is to be successful.

Situations like these call for the integration strategy to include coaching for parent company executives on how to make entry into the acquisition. It only takes a couple of false starts (e.g., confusion regarding reporting relationships and lines of authority) and the slightest display of arrogance or insensitivity for complications to develop. Westinghouse feels that its success in securing the long-term commitment of current owner/managers is directly proportioned to the amount of time it spends *during negotiations* on the following:

1. Talking to the owners about Westinghouse's expectations for the business.
2. Listening carefully to their stated expectations.
3. Discussing alternatives and contingencies.
4. Above all else, describing fully and fairly the management controls, procedures, delays, and frustrations they may encounter after Westinghouse assumes control.

MANAGEMENT HEADACHES

Management of virtually any business enterprise will find there is no shortage of problems to contend with at each stage of the organization's life cycle. Whether it be the start-up of a new venture, the struggle during the early years to establish a niche in the marketplace, the effort of a mature firm to fend off aggressive new competition, or the trials of managing mergers and acquisitions, the people in charge have their work cut out for them. But in making an acquisition, top executives not only end up buying someone else's problems, the merger event itself creates a host of new headaches, as well.

2

A Classification of Merger/ Acquisition Climates

A categorization of different merger/acquisition situations makes it much easier for management to anticipate the problems that are most likely to occur. Four quite distinct acquisitional postures can be identified (see Figure 2-1). Each one has its idiosyncrasies and has unique implications regarding how management should gear up to cope with the difficulties that routinely develop.

Figure 2-1 Acquisition postures

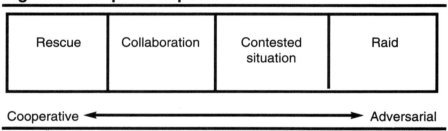

Rescue	Collaboration	Contested situation	Raid

Cooperative ⟵—————————————————⟶ Adversarial

The four broad categories of mergers are rescues, collaborations, contested situations, and raids. As Figure 2-1 shows, the rescue represents the most cooperative interface between acquirer and target company. At the other end of the continuum is the corporate raid, the most adversarial takeover situation. All four scenarios create adjustment problems for the acquisition. But the nature of the takeover determines to a large extent how severe the blow is, how long the trauma lasts, and the extent of damage to corporate health.

THE RESCUE

Actually, there are two different types of rescue operations. Frequently a rescue develops in response to a raid that has been initiated by another firm, sending the target company executives scurrying in search of a "white knight." The second type of rescue occurs as a financial salvage operation. In both situations, the to-be-acquired firm is casting about for help, looking for relief of some sort. The purchasing firm, therefore, is basically viewed as a welcome party. Still, there are almost always some mixed feelings on the part of the firm being acquired. Being rescued ordinarily is just the lesser of two evils and is not what the target company would choose if it had any good alternatives.

Looking for Daddy Warbucks. The organization problems and management actions in the white knight scenario are very different from this situation. Here the acquired firm is on the brink of financial disaster, or at least suffering from a lack of key resources (usually monetary). The very nature of the problem suggests that the company has some significant weaknesses. There probably have been fundamental mistakes in the way the organization has been run. Incumbent management usually has to stand responsible for the negative state of affairs and thus is viewed as an unpromising cadre to turn things around.

Odds are the top management team in the acquisition has already taken its best shot at running the company. Otherwise the firm would not have gone looking for a financial savior in Daddy Warbucks. The obvious question then becomes, if these managers have been responsible for bringing their company to this dire point, and have proved incapable of overcoming problems of their own making, should they be entrusted with the husbandry of any new funds Daddy Warbucks is to invest in it? The acquiring organization may be quite flush, but who wants to throw good money after bad?

So in this rescue operation, quite a few members of the existing management team may be politely asked to leave. Naturally there is fear in the hearts of some executives when it becomes obvious that an unknown number of people occupying the management ranks will likely be replaced. Employees in the acquired firm sense an acute loss of leadership, too, as their familiar standard-bearers leave the scene. Employees are understandably threatened by the prospect that the new owner may choose to deal with the financial problems by such actions as selling off a division, shutting down a plant, doing away with two layers of management, or cutting back the overall work force by a large percentage. These are logical concerns.

This type of rescue is one of the two merger situations that require the most intervention by the parent firm. On one hand, people in the acquired company realize things have reached the point where there will be sacrifices to make to be merged by rescue. And the people in charge have decided that the trade-offs tilt in favor of being taken over by another organization. But there are always some employees who feel they would have been better served by not being acquired. They would prefer to stake their chances on surviving through alternative means. Thus, even the most benevolent Daddy Warbucks is likely to meet with varying levels of resistance in carrying out the financial rescue.

If the acquired firm was on its last financial leg, the rescue may generate a broadly felt sense of relief. Morale may improve. A new sense of challenge and anticipation may be apparent, and certainly should be capitalized on by the acquirer. But at the same time, the parent company should (1) gear up to cope with pockets of resistance and (2) be prepared to counteract feelings of excessive dependency on the part of some other personnel.

When a financially ailing company goes looking for Daddy Warbucks, the acquirer certainly needs to know the extent of its own resources. It needs to respect the limits of its ability to invest money and management in the new acquisition. Invariably, some type of rehabilitation, often a substantial degree of organization therapy, is required. So, although the rescued firm may come at a bargain price, it usually carries hefty risks as well.

In this rescue exercise, the two companies do cooperate to a high degree and enter into the merger by mutual preference. But the target company is still, in a sense, a vanquished firm. There are likely to be tender egos that result from this, together with a prevailing sense of defeat throughout the organization. In this atmosphere there is a critical need for Daddy Warbucks to do more than tighten things up financially or even throw some new money around. People in the acquired organization need help in rebuilding their corporate self-esteem. Their pride needs to be restored and their motivation regenerated. They need strong leadership and a well-defined sense of direction. And with all of this, the sooner the better.

Rescue by the White Knight. In this scenario we find the target company running for cover. It's a panic situation, and under careful scrutiny, the outcome usually carries the telltale signs of decisions based on expediency. Time pressures rarely permit adequate analysis of the situation, weighing the pros and cons, or searching for alternatives.

To get a quick gauge of the sort of problems this situation produces, think of it as involving impulse buying and panic selling.

To begin with, this suggests that many important issues get glossed over in both parties' haste to justify and finalize the deal.

And since there is such a shortage of data gathering and critical thought beforehand, there has to be much more of it after the purchase has been consummated.   When the smoke clears, permitting a more relaxed and objective appraisal of all aspects of the situation, the flaws in the fabric of the agreement become much more visible.   Now it's time for the selling firm to begin second-guessing the wisdom of moving so rashly in the direction of the new parent company.   Meanwhile, the white knight may begin to suffer buyer's remorse.

One of the biggest merger shoot-outs ever seen in the United States involved Conoco, Inc., Seagram, Mobil Oil Corporation and E. I. Dupont deNemours & Company. With two corporate raiders and a white knight involved, it appeared there was something for everybody. Certainly the stakes were high, but it was not a case where the winner took all.   Conoco scrambled to elude the corporate clutches of first Seagram and then of Mobil Oil, but the aftermath provided hard data that rescue has its own risks.   DuPont prevailed in its offer, only to find its own independence threatened by possible loss of control to Seagram.   Top management had to face a barrage of criticism from shareholders who were very irate about their sagging stock prices.   DuPont looked uneasily at its bankers and delicately pleaded for peace with Seagram, still a major stockholder.   Meanwhile Conoco employees began to reassess their careers and wonder who would be the first to go, as it was apparent that the new owner would be divesting certain parts of Conoco in an effort to improve the financial picture.

Certainly this type of rescue is likely to generate many post-merger surprises.   Quite a few significant issues that are not addressed or that are inadequately dealt with during the negotiations remain to be hammered out by the two firms.   Usually both the rescuer and the acquired firm find themselves having to make compromises nobody foresaw.   Ground rules that were not established regarding how the two firms will live together have to be determined.   And whereas before the papers were signed everybody seemed quite cooperative and eager to strike an agreement, now the gears seem to grind much more slowly and a far more cautious spirit prevails.

Often the management teams from both organizations feel

compelled to strengthen their respective firm's position, realizing they may have acted a bit rashly in their haste to make the deal acceptable to each other. The acquired firm, in particular, is prone to feel in retrospect that the new sense of safety came at too dear a cost. Personnel in the rescued company show an almost immediate transition from a sense of relief to wariness. Throughout the organization people begin to wonder, "What have we done?" Now that the fearsome threat of the corporate raider has been eliminated, increasing prominence is given to the new threat that the white knight will take advantage of the situation.

So the white knight rescue is a little too much like a weekend Reno marriage. Without the traditional courtship period where people (or companies) have more opportunity to get to know each other and work through important differences, the "little period of adjustment" that routinely goes with marriage can become a long, drawn-out, and gut-wrenching experience. It is worth remembering that quick marriages are typically the least successful, the hardest to make work.

In the aftermath of the white knight rescue there is a powerful need for top management to take steps that ensure the two organizations get to know each other. There will be a need to work through the many aspects of how the two companies will interact. This may point to the value of conducting compatibility studies of the two firms' different cultures, operating practices, and the like. Employee attitude surveys can be utilized to give a rapid, comprehensive assessment of how the rescued firm looks from the underbelly perspective. Undoubtedly top management needs to work hard to sell the idea of the acquisition to people in both companies. Finally, the white knight rescue needs to be viewed as one of the rare acquisitions where the parent company might well take a hands-off stance for an indefinite period of time. Certainly if the new acquisition is a successful, smoothly running operation, extreme care should be exercised in the way it is handled.

COLLABORATION

By far the biggest percentage of acquisitions would fall into this category. Someone wants to buy and the other company wants to sell or is persuaded to sell, so that both parties approach the bargaining table of their own choosing. It is not a situation like the rescue or raid, in particular, where one of the firms has its back to the wall and ends up with a new parent.

Other identifying characteristics of the collaboration are that the acquirer does not use surprise tactics on the target firm, nor is there use of heavy-handed measures. Rather, both parties strive to employ diplomacy, goodwill, and negotiating finesse in striking a deal that represents a fair exchange. Usually the negotiations are carried out with mutual respect and strong interest in doing business with each other.

These are important points, because with more goodwill going into the efforts in the negotiating stages, there is likely to be more of a positive atmosphere as the two companies come out of the deal. A top executive from Beatrice Foods describes how that firm pursued a collaborative approach in its acquisition program during the '60s and '70s:

> We only went after the friendly ones. If a guy said, "We don't want any part of you," we'd back away. Now we wouldn't give up. There are lot of them that we kept after. This stance paid dividends to us for this reason—we had people coming to us. We had built up a reputation where we treated people well and let them run their own deals. Now the bigger deals were ones where we took the initiative. We approached them. But many of those companies joined us because of our reputation for fair treatment and letting them run their own shows.

Beatrice seems to have judiciously weighed the pros and cons of the various acquisition tactics and decided to follow the straight and narrow path of collaboration. This sort of merger/acquisition scenario provides a pretty respectable base from which to build. There will be some ambivalence or mixed feelings on the part of the firm being acquired, but overall the positives are viewed as outweighing the negatives. Collaboration is a pretty nonadversarial situation.

Why is it then that employee concerns are still so much of a problem? For one thing, the people at the top may be sold on the deal while nobody ever takes the pains necessary to sell it to the people below. It may represent a win-win proposition for the two companies, but top management should never assume that this is understood by people who have not been privy to the negotiating sessions wherein the agreement was engineered.

It is almost impossible to overcommunicate in the merger arena. Obviously, top management must employ discretion and a careful sense of timing in the handling of certain information, and it is risky to make very many promises or strong statements. But apart from that, usually the more information that can be shared, the better. It is difficult to find a company in the stages of being acquired that could not benefit from a better communication process.

Collaborative mergers and acquisitions are often jarring experiences because of poor follow-up management. In other words, while there was good negotiation, there is bad integration. The delicate footwork manifested in the sensitive process of making the deal disappears. Parent company management may breathe a sigh of relief with the opportunity to get back to "business as usual." But people in the acquired firm know it's a new ball game. They are like a raw nerve with regard to how they are being handled by the new owner, who so characteristically quits tiptoeing too soon.

Collaboration ordinarily involves the most courtship. In fact, the pacing is part of the collaboration itself. As a well-known executive in one of the country's most acquisition-minded conglomerates has said, "Timing is everything." If the acquirer pushes too hard, a raid can develop. The timing has to please both parties, and as a rule, intensive efforts go into talking through the marriage plus the plans for the postmerger relationship. Generally speaking, collaboration—more than any of the other categories—is a merger condition in which the autonomy of the acquired company is most likely to be preserved.

Usually there is less need for intervention on the part of the parent. Thus, in this merger situation, the conditions are most appropriate for "management deals," contractual arrangements which are designed to retain key executives.

Because of these practices, the mergers that come about through collaboration typically suffer the least from "postmerger drift," the customary sag in productivity, morale, and operating effectiveness. Both parties to the merger have more ownership of the decision and therefore more commitment to making it all work.

This also suggests, however, that the acquired firm could be quite resistant to changes or interventions designed unilaterally by the new owner. Such intervention is usually perceived as an oppressive, inequitable move which violates the collaborative spirit that first gave rise to the merger. It is somewhat ironic in that the collaborative precedent established early on hints that this is the way the two firms are going to relate as time goes by. But it is unlikely that the parent company management will want (or be able) to interact with the acquisition in a collaborative manner under all circumstances. So when the precedent is not followed, management in the new acquisition gets jumpy as well as defensive. Since lower level people in the acquisition are watching their superiors like hawks, they too begin to resonate with the same negative vibrations. This sort of "collaboration backlash" is a phenomenon acquirers will find almost impossible to avoid entirely.

THE CONTESTED SITUATION

The distinguishing difference between this acquisition approach and collaboration is that here only one of the two parties has a strong interest in making the deal, or the two firms want very different deals. Also, a contested situation may develop when there are multiple suitors who keep upping the ante for a target company. Often the firm under consideration is a reluctant bride, but is unable to successfully defend itself against a takeover.

In this scenario, the negotiating can become very aggressive. There is plenty of resistance, but it is more depersonalized than that found in the raid. Here the battling between the two firms remains more logic–based and not so emotional as it is in the raid.

Probably the major difference between these two most adversarial takeovers, though, is that in the contested situation there is less of a feeling that there is a victor and a vanquished. It is common for both parties to walk away basically content with the deal that is struck. In that regard it remains primarily a win-win encounter, and the aftermath reflects an important spirit of cooperation. There well may be a strong flavor of opportunism in the behavior of both sides to the merger equation. But in contrast to the raid, the contested situation gives management in the target company a much better chance to emerge as heroes rather than as martyrs or losers.

By the time the deal has been finalized, however, the troops in the acquired firm often are quite battle weary. The bidding contest that marks this merger fray can be very stressful and unsettling. Ambiguity mounts quickly, and employees have a tendency to lose their job concentration as they watch all the fireworks. Concern for their own careers can become quite intense if a company vying for control implies that a takeover would be followed by divestitures, shutdowns, consolidations, or layoffs. The contested situation and the raid are both merger types that bring about a slowdown in productivity and organizational momentum even *before* a deal is consummated. So usually in these two acquisition battles the people problems have a head start on management.

The bidding process for the Chicago *Sun-Times* created precisely this kind of turmoil. A local investor group headed by James Hogue (the incumbent publisher) saw its offer being shunned in favor of a higher bid by Australian publisher Rupert Murdoch. A few months earlier the owners had stated that Murdoch would be an unacceptable bidder, but apparently his higher offer proved to be a persuasive argument. Still a third would-be buyer emerged at the last minute with an even higher bid, but that overture got a cool reception. As the acquisition contest wore on, employees first became distracted, then worried about major staff cutbacks that were rumored, and finally openly critical of the impending sale to Murdoch. Pessimism led to a wait-and-see attitude and fomented a rapidly building atmosphere of resistance throughout the work force.

Contested acquisitions, together with some rescues and most raids, generate enough stir to get quite a bit of attention. Frequently, a few of the heads that are turned belong to executive recruiters. And in all the commotion of a contested situation or a raid, in particular, the search consultant often finds several high-talent executives with a rapidly growing interest in considering career opportunities elsewhere. This can help create a talent drain and leadership vacuum that cripple the acquired firm's effectiveness in the postmerger environment.

THE RAID

Probably nobody would choose the hostile takeover route as a preferred method for making an acquisition. Now and then an executive may be invigorated by the thrill of the chase, and it can feel good to come out on top. But the headaches usually outweigh the ego gratifications.

In this merger scenario, the adversarial climate is at its peak, with the result being maximum resistance on the part of the target firm. Typically, an intense emotional component is interjected into the battle for ownership. Often the defense becomes desperate. The propaganda mills in both companies pump out charges and counter-charges. It is bad enough that accurate communication is a scarce commodity even in the most benevolent acquisition environment. Here the truth gets stretched ridiculously out of shape and the rumor mill roars out of control.

A routine practice is for management in the besieged organization to generate strong antagonism among its employees toward the corporate raider. Invariably, the employees seem to love it. They defiantly wave their own corporate flag, rallying behind their leaders and becoming even more cohesive in the struggle against a common, outside enemy. This interesting phenomenon occurred in response to the LTV Corporation's $450 million tender offer for Grumman Aerospace Corporation. Grumman lived up to its label as a defense company in rapidly fortifying its position. The first step taken by target company management was to proclaim that the merger would have a disruptive effect on employees, hurt morale, and create an uncertain future for the firm. Then Grumman went even further, soliciting reinforcements from every other conceivable source—e.g., politicians, judges, employees, public sentiment, even the company's pension plan. This counterattack worked for Grumman, but a similar effort by Continental Air Lines, Inc. failed to fend off Texas International Company. The latter merger fight was a draining, expensive, bitterly fought eight-month duel. And though Texas International won the battle, the war obviously was not over. Next came the subtle resistance, the guerrilla warfare in the corporate underground.

It is true, however, that when this sort of defense works it can be a very positive event for the target company. A more intense corporate spirit develops and management emerges with stronger backing from the employees than it had before the raid commenced. Workers swell with enhanced pride and morale ordinarily notches up.

The target company's executives can almost always whip up strong employee concern and bitter resistance to the takeover. The risk inherent in this defense tactic is substantial, though, as the warnings top management gives to its work force can be a self-fulfilling prophecy if the hostile takeover is successfully accomplished by the raider. The scary scenarios target company executives develop in playing to their people's fears are potential attitudinal monsters—management's creation, they sometimes become management's curse.

When the fierce defense fails, there are many problems that develop out of the residual antipathy. The hard-fought battles usually leave behind a lot of wreckage. Employees cannot make the psychological shifts that would be necessary to go blithely from battle to brotherhood in a few days.

The raid creates winners and losers, but it does not necessarily end the fight. Long after the legal documents have been signed and media attention has faded away, the war may continue. So there is a catch-22 to the corporate raid, and it goes like this—acquiring a company to sustain growth and nurture the corporate base, when undertaken through hostile action, creates negative management conditions that actually hamper expansion. The defense designed to ward off a corporate raider does not vanish in the event that it fails. The mine field planted to protect against the acquirer remains to plague management in both companies.

Top management in the newly acquired firm finds itself in somewhat of a box. Having led a very antagonistic, emotional battle against the company that is now the new parent organization, the management team that has been taken over must either recant, thereby losing credibility, or resign. In either event, the leadership of the acquired company is in trouble. As in war, the leader of a conquered nation must try to alleviate the enmity and adversarial climate that he has orchestrated. The other alternative is to abdicate leadership.

In corporate wars, the best and brightest often flee to friendlier settings. Talent leaves first in the aftermath of hostile acquisitions, and these organizational refugees may leave behind only a shell of a management team and a work force plagued by resentment and uncertainty. Even in amiable acquisitions, "people problems" rank right up at the top along with negative economic conditions as a prime reason for merger tangles. Resisted takeovers are even more prone to human-resource failure.

Top management in the parent company also finds itself in some operational straight jackets. On one hand, there is a need for fence mending. But because the newly acquired managers and employees are somewhat recalcitrant and begrudging, they require more policing. So the raider is often compelled to impose tighter controls and send in its own managers to function as "occupation troops." That can further alienate and demoralize target company personnel, however, resulting in management bailouts and sabotaged productivity. Corporate raiders might wish to bolster morale by promising their new corporate roommates that "management will not be changed, things will remain the same, it will be business as usual." It would be nice if things could operate like that, because in hostile takeovers employees are especially sensitive to restructuring. But it is the very thing they make more necessary by their unwillingness to adapt.

The raiding company implicitly sets a management philosophy through the way in which it captures its quarry. In essence, the raider has made a "corporate intervention" even before it actually succeeds in the takeover. A management policy has already been demonstrated by the acquirer. Thus, it becomes very difficult to collaborate after the raid has been carried out. Management in the parent company is making a very hollow statement when it assures everyone that "we don't plan to make any changes." In reality, the changes have already begun. The target company has to make quick changes in some of its behavior because of the acquisition threat. And the premerger climate virtually guarantees that further changes will be forthcoming in the postmerger period.

THE INCLINE OF RESISTANCE

The degree of resistance to the acquisition becomes greater as one moves from a relatively cooperative merger to the more adversarial events. The incline of resistance demonstrates (1) the intensity of opposition to the other party's merger objectives and (2) the amount of resources (money, energy, time, etc.) expended struggling with the merger event (see Figure 2-2).

Figure 2-2 The incline of resistance

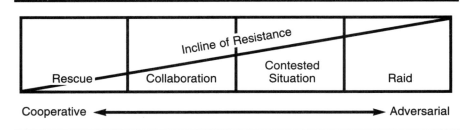

Both the acquirer and the acquiree demonstrate forces of resistance which range from negligible to extreme. A company being rescued, as a whole, usually welcomes the acquirer. Even within the rescue, however, there will be at least passive resistance to doing things a new way. Furthermore, some people in the target firm will invariably oppose the idea of running into the arms of Daddy Warbucks or a white knight.

The incline of resistance peaks out in the hostile, defensive environment of a raid, and parent company management needs to be able and ready to meet this challenge. Obviously, much more will be required of parent company management in acquisitions where the incline of resistance is most pronounced. A collaborative acquisition might prove to be a successful venture where a hostile takeover of the same firm would lead to failure.

As the incline mounts, both initial negotiation strategies and eventual integration policies must change. The more resistance increases, the more people on each side become one-sided. That is, they become more attached to and have more personally invested in their particular side of the issues. This is just one of the common sociological aspects of mergers and acquisitions.

The higher the incline of resistance goes because of the nature of the acquisition environment, the longer it usually takes for that resistance to subside. Raids and contested situations usually involve the most prolonged postmerger period of opposition. Those two types of takeovers call for the most concerted efforts by parent company management to alleviate the problems. Ordinarily a one-shot attempt will not be sufficient to overcome the polarization and adversarial hangover that remains. Instead, management should design a strategic integration program that respects the magnitude of the problems and that holds promise for getting people from both firms to the point of pulling together for the good of the merged firms.

THE RISK CURVE

While the incline of resistance steadily increases from the rescue type of acquisition through the raid situation, the amount of financial risk that management has to contend with tends to be greater at each end of the acquisitional continuum. In the rescue, the acquirer gains a firm which is often beset by financial woes and possesses a dearth of leadership.

The raid situation almost guarantees overt resistance and threat of bailouts by the most capable people within the organization. At a time when top talent is needed to stabilize a company acquired through hostile action, those people look elsewhere for career opportunities.

In the rescue event it is less likely that people will leave. Unfortunately, incompetent individuals who have created the conditions necessitating a rescue are sometimes difficult to dismiss. Rather than demonstrating explicit hostility toward the acquirer, companies being rescued often have a work force characterized by passivity and inertia. And just as that contingent of people demonstrated a prior inability to turn things around on their own, they frequently prove to have real difficulty adapting to the needed changes once new

Figure 2-3 The risk curve

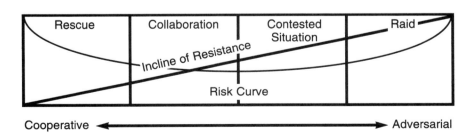

management takes over.

The risk curve (see Figure 2-3) may be misleading on one point—all acquisitions involve financial risk.   Collaborative or contested acquisitions can result in financial failures, just as can rescues or raids. This curve assumes that, all things being equal with regard to the external economic climate, the risks of failure are greater with the rescue or raid situation than they are with either of the other two merger classifications.

Corporate raiders often have to spend more than would be desired to obtain a reluctant firm, and thus become financially threatened by the debt burden that must be assumed. Also, the resistance gradient is at its highest point in the raiding scenario, and employee resistance can sabotage even a fairly well-financed takeover. In the more cooperative rescue mode, risk is great because of the nature of the takeover. It often involves saving a company which is flirting with insolvency or which must shore up sagging or departing leadership. The vitality of such a firm is seriously in question.

NEGATIVE SYNERGY OF MERGERS

A common argument offered in favor of mergers and acquisitions is that a positive synergistic linkup can be achieved. Company A buys Company B, and their combined resources represent more than the sum of their individual parts. The synergistic sword cuts both ways, however, and the downside risks typically are not explored in as much depth as the upside potential.

Regrettably, two companies' problems can be just as synergistic as their potentials. One firm's difficulties plus the ailments of the other cannot be conveniently added up to a neat sum total. The merger brings with it a new and unique set of previously nonexistent difficulties.

Over the years, top-management teams have been prone to disregard the negative synergy of mergers in their strategic planning relative to growth by acquisition. Corporate planners focus their analysis primarily on what the buyer and the target company can each bring to the merger, with little formal study being aimed toward ascertaining what the merger event itself will do. In fact, the merger is a corporate intervention. It should be respected as a new force management must contend with. At times it stands as a rather cataclysmic influence. When the decision to acquire or merge is first being made, those realities do not exist. But newly forged corporate bonds bring new realities and a fresh set of facts.

Management in the acquiring company should take pains to play out various merger scenarios in careful detail. More thought and war gaming should be devoted to an analysis of how the companies can be combined. Contingency planning should be expanded to take into fuller account the negative synergy that may develop.

This is particularly true in the corporate raid, because in the hostile takeover the two parties are not working together in a collaborative fashion at all. They are not putting their heads together to figure out how to make the deal work. Thus, contingency planning is extremely one-sided. The acquiring company—and for that matter, the target company as well—must lean much too heavily on conjecture. It is bad enough if the adversary does not work *with* you. In the raid he is working *against* you. Each party to the merger throws surprises into the situation. Each company is at odds with the other's line of reasoning. Both parties are out to confound the other's strategies.

Ordinarily, merger planning and decision making are based most heavily on the financial considerations involved. But the success or failure hinges very heavily on the intentions of both sides in the equation. And in a hostile takeover attempt, neither one of the management teams has sufficient insight into the intentions of the other. This makes it extremely difficult to predict what's coming.

3

Psychological Shockwaves of Mergers and Acquisitions

When merger rumblings are heard in the organizational jungle, the natives get restless. The work climate changes. This change is a given. It is not something that top management in the acquiring firm can allow or prevent at will. The magnitude of change can be controlled to some extent. But whether or not there is change at all simply is not subject to debate. Everyone who will be affected by the merger/acquisition—and top management in particular—should accept this fact and concentrate on how to come to grips with it.

Effective management of mergers and acquisitions demands that the people in charge be prepared for the emotional shake-up accompanying this kind of organizational growth. When word goes out that an acquisition is in the wind, there is a measurable impact on employee attitudes, feelings, and work behavior. The regrettable fact is that these shifts or changes—again, unavoidable—are for the most part negative. They reflect how a distressing psychological event has affected the lives of executives, managers, and the rank and file. Usually people in both companies, but particularly the one being acquired, must go through a major adjustment process. They have to adapt to a variety of new organizational realities.

But people often resist change. Changes they fear or changes that are not of their own making ordinarily will elicit the most resistance. This is a key point, because most people whose company has merged or been acquired had no part in that decision. Not only did they have no say in the matter, they often were taken completely by surprise.

Employees are blindsided, emotionally jolted, by the news that their corporate family is being reshaped and given a new authority structure. This is somewhat like a child being hit cold with the word that a new parent is entering the family structure, and maybe the existing parent is leaving the scene altogether. Rather disconcerting news, obviously, and certain to arouse extreme anxiety along with a variety of other unpleasant feelings.

Like the child who has just been "sold out" by the parent, commonly in a surprise move, employees usually feel no personal ownership of the decision someone made to merge or sell the company. Thus, the employees' commitment to support the idea may be very weak.

The heightened state of uncertainty that is instantly created pervades the work climate. People get jumpy. They wonder when the other shoe will fall. And because they fear additional surprises—particularly some regarding their own career safety—they move instinctively to protect themselves.

The merger and the potential changes it brings are resisted deliberately as well as unconsciously. Some people are very outspoken and overt in expressing their dismay. Instead of trying to conceal their opposition, they purposefully ventilate it, perhaps in hopes of short-circuiting the deal. Sometimes people choose to be very open in expressing their shock, anger, and frustration, while some employees could not hide their feelings even if they tried.

The unconscious resistance, far more subtle but oftentimes more pernicious and damaging in the scheme of things, is much more widespread. It is more passive in nature. It is manifested in the job performance of people who would honestly assert that they wish to be cooperative and support the corporate marriage. But the hard facts argue convincingly that the unconscious resistance is there, and that it is taking its toll. It shows in morale, turnover statistics, productivity, loss of competitive advantage, deterioration in revenues, disappointing profits, etc.

Even when people in the acquired firm make a concerted effort to adjust and embrace it, the merger can turn sour. Their coping behaviors tend to be highly self-oriented and thus dysfunctional as far as the organizational good is concerned. The things they do and don't do in looking out for themselves are frequently incompatible with what the organization needs from them at that point in time. Much employee behavior that is well intentioned and even self-sacrificing runs counter to what needs to happen in a merger environment. But if management has not been trained to manage the change process, why should they be expected to play it by ear and get it right the first time around? Or even the second, third, or fourth time?

KEY DYNAMICS SET IN MOTION BY THE MERGER

The merger/acquisition scenario is highly predictable in terms of the psychological dynamics that are generated. It helps if management knows this and knows what to expect. That is at least a first step in the direction of being much better equipped to deal with the situation effectively.

The shudder that moves through an organization when it is acquired is no peculiar or unique phenomenon. It is simply human nature in action. And since organizations are made up of people, the key dynamics can be anticipated with great certainty by top management.

Ambiguity

As the dust begins to settle following the announcement of an impending acquisition, a powerful new force begins to register its influence. This first dynamic is a climate of ambiguity. It is manifested in a work atmosphere wherein there are far more questions than answers. People at all levels feel it as an information vacuum. There is a disconcerting lack of clarity regarding the corporate future and the further surprises or changes it holds. People also wonder about the role they as employees may or may not play in the upcoming scheme of things. Even if higher management tries to alleviate this uneasiness by giving assurances about job tenure, a substantial amount of tension remains as people wonder about what new requirements might be made of them, what new reporting relationships may develop, and so on. Employees generally suspect there will be some sort of change in procedures, objectives, operating style, and the management structure.

This pervasive ambiguity stems quite naturally from two different roots: (1) top management's need (or felt need) to be discreet and (2) top management's own lack of definite, specific facts regarding the impact and various ramifications of the merger.

Everybody is suffering from the unknown. And the truth is that even the president and board of directors do not have it within their power to satisfy everyone's curiosity and rid the work environment of the ambiguity. Furthermore, top executives usually consider it injudicious, possibly unkind, and maybe even illegal to inform people of the hard facts in many situations.

So a great deal of ambiguity, vagueness, or fuzziness builds up as the merger/acquisition situation unfolds. Some people have a psychological makeup that enables them to endure this kind of work climate reasonably well. Others find it extremely upsetting. Those employees who like order, generous job structure, a well-defined and predictable chain of command, and a clear sense of direction are inclined to feel dangerously adrift in the merger environment. All of a sudden their world has become destabilized.

Weakening Trust Level

The second major dynamic that needs to be understood by top management is the lowered trust level in the company. Invariably, the announcement of merger plans will cause the affected parties to become more suspicious and wary.

One reason for this may be the rude shock often caused by the abrupt announcement of the merger. Employees quite understandably will often conclude that top management cannot be relied on to be sufficiently open and aboveboard about things that very directly affect the individual. Moreover, people at all strata in the corporate structure usually realize that the top decision makers know more than they are telling. Employees know implicitly that more surprises are forthcoming.

Personnel who previously were willing to give the company the benefit of the doubt now become skeptics, some even cynics. And those who were mistrustful or insecure to begin with may become downright antagonistic and paranoid. Those who had been quite willing to rely on top management to look out for the needs and interests of the average employee now feel obliged to change their perspective. Now everything that is done or said by key executives is viewed with a more jaundiced eye.

Actually, this is a rational response. It is a monster created (and sometimes unnecessarily nurtured) by top management in the way communications are handled and the degree of candor. The bigger the initial shock and the greater the secretiveness, the more the trust level suffers. This leads to the third dynamic.

Self-preservation

Merger/acquisition activity leads to self-preservation as a dominant motive in employee behavior. The weaker the trust level, the more visible are the self-protective behaviors that surface. Particularly those in the middle management and executive ranks begin to deploy their personal armaments toward maximum protection of their individual careers. Rank-and-file employees may be just as troubled as those in leadership positions, but usually they give much less visible evidence of attempts to protect their jobs.

It is interesting to observe the myriad ways in which people strive to defend themselves. Some launch an aggressive attack, actively vying for position, and sometimes hoping to leverage themselves strategically into a position of even greater power and prestige. Others lie low and wait for the smoke to clear, preferring to maneuver carefully rather than attack boldly. And some calculate their best odds as being to survive simply by not offending. They deliberately move out of the line of fire and hope that fate smiles on them.

At any rate, self-protective behaviors result in many "hidden agendas," and these divert time and energy from the pursuit of company objectives. Also, top management finds it more difficult to direct an effective corporate offensive because all of a sudden it is much harder to predict what people will do. Employee behavior is founded much more on emotion and obscure motives, while less on apparent logic or rational thought.

THE EMOTIONAL IMPACT ON PEOPLE

Human beings instinctively seek to maintain control and predictability over their world and their immediate environment. The more ambiguous the work climate is, as in a merger, the more this human goal is sabotaged. High levels of ambiguity lead to excessive uncertainty. Employees become confused, less sure of themselves, and sometimes highly anxious.

Even after the initial impact of the shock has diminished, employees in the acquired firm are hit with repeated demands for change and adaptation. This invariably disrupts their established and previously successful adjustment to life as they are beset by financial concerns, professional insecurities, and fear of the new as well as the unknown. These uncertainties, fears, and inner tensions do distinct damage to individual productivity. Regrettably, anxiety tends not to be a very constructive emotion. It inhibits creativity, interferes with one's ability to concentrate, acts as a drain on physical energy, and frequently lowers the person's frustration tolerance. Logical thought processes give way to emotionally colored problem solving and decision making.

The impact of a lowered trust level within the corporation is similarly negative. This, too, can provoke an unhealthy degree of anxiety. Tension mounts, contributing to the psychological stress load employees have to carry. Individuals may become more fearful or noticeably more angry, hostile, and defensive. Employee morale and attitudes are corrupted by this highly contagious mindset that ravages the workplace.

When self-preservation becomes a primary concern, employee behavior reflects selfishness at the expense of a needed concern for the organizational good. Those personnel who suffer a sense of betrayal by top management commonly transfer their loyalties. The owner or CEO who may have been an important father figure for the organization may come to be viewed as one who abandoned his people, the implication being that one is foolish to place trust in top management (particularly if top management consists of new outsiders).

Sometimes these self-protective behaviors lead to a variety of regressive acts on the part of employees. For example, some people withdraw. A manager may hole up in his office. Employees may find superiors more inaccessible, and may themselves invest less effort in communicating. Workers often exhibit a greater degree of emotional detachment vis-á-vis the firm. Thus, their commitment weakens and, along with it, standards drop and output diminishes. But detachment does represent one way of protecting oneself from being taken advantage of, hurt, or surprised.

In some instances an entire department or work group becomes more close-knit as far as its own members are concerned, yet more isolated from the organizational effort as a whole.

The important thing for management (in both the acquiring and acquired firms) to remember is that these are all legitimate reactions. Obviously they are counterproductive and do a disservice to the organization, and they frequently create even greater problems for the employee. But they are understandable and predictable in view of the key dynamics that underlie them.

NEGATIVE EFFECTS ON EMPLOYEE BEHAVIOR

As the psychological shockwaves surge through the organization, they take their toll in operating effectiveness. Emotions—psychological factors—begin to bias behavior. Six major problem areas highlight the fact that top management is making a crucial error when it fails to deal expertly with the emotional issues in a merger or acquisition.

Communication Deteriorates

As the trust level in the organization drops, people begin to play their cards much closer to their chest. The information channels receive less input that is dependable. And the data that is submitted is more likely to be filtered, distorted, or edited out completely before it reaches its intended destinations.

It seems that virtually everyone has an increased appetite for information and a diminished willingness to feed honest, accurate data to others. Rumors and speculation rush in to fill the communication vacuum that develops. There is no overall shortage of information, but much of what is there in abundance is erroneous and/or verbal clutter.

This problem of information warp is compounded by people's exaggeration, fear mongering, and wishful thinking. Many silly notions are passed along from person to person, frequently embellished with each retelling. The traditional rules of gossip prevail—that is, truth gets distorted, unfounded ideas are reported as established facts, insignificant matters come to sound like high drama, problems are blown out of proportion, etc. Some people intentionally twist the truth and circulate erroneous information. Their motive may be to sandbag higher management, sabotage a peer they see as a potential competitor, or protect themselves and perhaps justify their mistakes.

The rampant mistrust, wariness, and paranoia cause people to distort a lot of what they see and hear. As people become more skeptical and cynical regarding the validity of what higher management has to say, they are inclined to misinterpret and misperceive far more than they would under ordinary circumstances. Issues are emotionalized, and that contributes to data distortion. People lose objectivity as a result of their concern and ego-involvement.

Top management is likely to experience frustration regardless of how honest it tries to be in communicating with employees at the various levels in the firm. To some extent this is because people selectively perceive. Some hear only what they want to hear or what they expect to be told. Others construe beyond what top management actually says, reading between the lines and in the process reading more into a statement than was originally intended. Hints, subtle implications, or innuendos are mentally snatched up, fleshed out in much greater detail by the person's imagination, and then thrown back in the face of the executive later on as proof of his lack of integrity. It is very common to observe employees mentally constructing the reality (1) they wish for or (2) they fear.

It is ironic that top management probably never does try harder to be so truthful than it does in the merger/acquisition arena, and yet still fails. There should be little doubt that top management genuinely wants to tell the truth. But frequently executives may not know what the truth is and, as a result, catch themselves (or get caught) in duplicity. It is important to remember that employees commonly are not feeling very congenial toward the owners and top executives after the announcement that an acquisition is forthcoming. Employees are expecting more trouble. And they are expecting more surprises from the people in charge. Furthermore, when the top executives talk, everyone else in the organization hangs onto their every word. It is easy for the boss to make communication mistakes.

At any rate, because of the facades, faking, outright lies, and inadvertent misunderstandings, the organizational trust level is still further diminished. Weakening trust, in turn, causes more communication damage, and the downward spiral continues.

There are other reasons for communication difficulties that develop a little further along in the takeover process. First, the communication networks tend to become more complex. More people become involved in problem solving and decision making, and this blurs the issue regarding who should be informed regarding what. Also, the communication channels typically grow longer. The distances from decision centers increase. A company traditionally may have had the benefit of an owner/operator who was always available and easily accessible for information or decisions. But if the company is sold to an acquirer with home offices 2,000 miles away, it is going to become more difficult and time-consuming to transact business. As information begins to travel along different paths, it also becomes easy for some people to unintentionally get left out of the loop. This can result in the loss of crucial input, and also will frequently give rise to backtracking and regrouping to get things coordinated. Finally, companies involved in the merger process often discover that they communicate in somewhat different languages. That would be enough of a problem in itself, but remember that the people in the acquired firm (or both firms, perhaps, if a full merger is to be accomplished) are suffering the additional communication problems associated with the emotional trauma they are experiencing.

Perhaps the worst thing about communication problems is that they don't just remain communication problems. They create secondary symptoms that then must be addressed.

Productivity Suffers and Momentum Sags

With self-preservation becoming a more paramount concern in the minds of employees, they become less willing to make decisions or take risks. There is an air of tentativeness or a wait-and-see attitude that prevails. Managers and upper-level executives often move into holding patterns, deliberately choosing a play-it-safe stance. Everybody seems to feel more comfortable with the idea of making sins of omission rather than commission. Employees seem more willing to do nothing than to do wrong.

Part of the productivity loss can be attributed to people's resistance to change. Upon close scrutiny, some of that resistance actually makes pretty good sense. Employees throughout the organization simply may not know what changes are required. (Here is a good example of where the communication processes may have failed.) Others choose not to exercise initiative, possibly not even to act very vigorously on definite instructions, simply because they don't know why something is being required. People hesitate to embrace new work roles or tackle new assignments due to uncertainty regarding their own ability to make the changes. Finally, the problem is still further compounded by people not having a good understanding regarding the standards by which they will be judged.

So the big question in people's minds appears to be "Whom do I need to please?" Until that has been determined and employees have ascertained to their own satisfaction what it takes to please that person or make marks in that score book, little is going to happen. People assume a more conservative stance and are most comfortable living with the status quo.

Effective management, then, means making the acquired work force feel secure enough to remain active, decisive, and resourceful. It means providing a good sense of direction and explaining the rationale for the course that has been charted. Finally, it means letting people know who's keeping score and how it's being kept, plus demonstrating that they have the encouragement and support of parent company management.

Parochialism Increases and Team Play Deteriorates

The merger environment frequently sees intergroup cooperation and support being sacrificed for a better defended self or a less vulnerable in-group. This, of course, is a direct outgrowth of the lowered trust level and desire for self-preservation. If the takeover is non-hostile, and particularly if there is to be very little or no consolidating or eliminating of functions, things may proceed smoothly. But it is not unusual to find one department or work group seeking to further its cause at the expense of another. The "we" spirit can evaporate in an atmosphere where people concentrate more on tooting their own horns or protecting their flanks.

Sometimes team play suffers more within than between teams. This happens when an employee decides that individual effort is a more promising avenue than team play for making it under the new regime that is to be established. Intragroup cohesiveness may be thrown to the winds, replaced by the feeling that it is every man for himself. In that atmosphere, individual cunning displaces collaborative effort.

Postmerger studies frequently find that tasks or projects requiring mutual effort and team play have bogged down in organizational politics. Competition subverts cooperative interplay and the overall corporate offensive suffers severely because of this splintering effect.

Power Struggles Throw Work into Disarray

At its best, a merger causes existing power networks to be reexamined and, in many instances, renegotiated. At its worst, a merger situation may deteriorate into a free-for-all as positions of authority are up for grabs. Sometimes long-standing alliances are dissolved altogether. And the old, established ways of getting things accomplished in the company simply may not work any longer.

Typically there is some jockeying for position. The natural result is that some people lose clout. And this dilemma helps explain why employees move into holding patterns.

The employee witnessing a shake-up in the power structure usually has some tough questions to face. For example, whose coat-tails shall he or she ride? Whose star is on the rise? Which programs will survive and which ones will go out the window?

Often there is much wasted effort. One person's pet project may lose its funding in the final stages, just when the real payoff is about to be realized. Another program may be sabotaged because its sponsor loses his or her power base in the organization. Many corporate opportunities slip past, disregarded or completely unnoticed, because managers are preoccupied with the infighting and intramural power plays.

One of the most common complaints of managers and executives whose firm has been acquired relates to their loss of autonomy and control. The adjustment can be very difficult to make. And until the power balance has been restructured, communicated, and actually accepted by lower-echelon personnel, organizational functioning cannot help but suffer. Unclear reporting relationships and poorly defined decision-making authority are familiar symptoms in mergers that go bad. And such problems plague, to some extent, almost all companies that find themselves being acquired by another organization.

Commitment is Lost

Corporate goals and objectives ordinarily become more obscure during the period immediately preceding and following the actual merger.   Even departmental objectives tend to become more indefinite, particularly in those work groups that can most likely see themselves being consolidated, reshaped, or eliminated altogether. This leads to a weakened sense of direction on the part of employees and that, in turn, results in diminished commitment. Employees rarely maintain a strong drive and desire to achieve when their targets are out of focus. When the game plan gets fuzzy, as it ordinarily does in the company that has just been acquired, the players simply don't play with the same degree of intensity.

For lack of a well-orchestrated, focused effort, employee energies are diffused.   The overall organization begins to drift because its various parts are not operating in a sufficiently purposeful, coordinated effort. In fact, one department or work group may be duplicating the efforts of another or, worse still, working at cross purposes. Management needs to remember that resources tend to gravitate toward clear goals. And if there is no well-defined sense of direction, then the available resources—personnel, money, material, and time— will inevitably be underutilized and spent in ways that fall well short of producing the potential returns.

There is still another important reason for the loss of commitment that occurs on the heels of an acquisition. Employees are inclined to assume that the corporation has become preoccupied with its financial best interests rather than their individual or collective being. So they are inclined to grow more blasé, with their dedication and loyalty deteriorating as the natural consequence.   Frequently their leader has left the scene, too, so that the personal ties which engendered loyalty and commitment have been severed.

In its worst form, a true adversarial relationship begins to fester. People may come to perceive this as a situation where it is "me against the company." Employees routinely look at a merger as an essential financial proposition rather than something that is done out of corporate humanitarianism. And their reaction, understandably, is to shift from having a company commitment to more of a self commitment. In the process, of course, motivation is further eroded.

Employees Bail Out

The sixth major people problem created by the psychological shockwaves is the "bailing out" phenomenon. The degree to which this occurs will depend heavily on the nature of the acquisition—e.g whether it was a mutually sought deal or fiercely resisted. Usually the more antagonistic the premerger battle, the more (and the quicker) people hotfoot it out of the acquisition toward other career opportunities.

Some people scramble just to get out before the axe falls. They may view the merger as their certain demise because it means the loss of a mentor and their own "favored person" status. Some bail out because they recognize a talented counterpart in the other firm and conclude that they personally will be the one to be let go because of duplicated functions. Others may take the initiative and leave because they anticipate obvious departmental consolidations that would make their talents superfluous.

Sometimes, however, employees leave simply to escape the increasing ambiguity and intense anxiety the merger generates for them personally. Once again, some people find it absolutely unbearable having to contend with a heightened state of ambiguity in their work. For these people, there is truth in the saying that "the certainty of misery is better than the misery of uncertainty." In other words, better to bail out into the fire immediately than sizzle in the frying pan indefinitely. This may not make sense to the objective observer, but if emotional logic exists, perhaps it is the rationale for this sort of behavior.

Often there are people who leave even though they personally feel very secure regarding the opportunity to keep their jobs. Their motivation can be that they envision a bleak future as they see the new corporate direction beginning to materialize. A manager in the acquired firm may lament that the company has been taken over by an outfit sure to redirect the organization away from his or her fundamental career interests. Another executive or manager may fear that the organization will be milked as a cash cow by the new parent company, thus drained of its resources and humbled before the eyes of the business world. Another person may worry about having a career stymied by a variety of new faces in superior positions or peer slots where they would be due an earlier promotion.

Some, of course, leave because they dislike the specter of encroaching controls. Faced with the possibility that they may suffer a loss of authority and decision-making latitude, they take the initiative, call it quits, and head in search of greener pastures. Sometimes it is not because they fear a loss of authority, but rather because they anticipate having to adapt to different (and unpalatable) operating philosophies after the merger.

Probably the most damaging bailouts are of those executives, managers, or technical experts who resign because they do not like the prospect of being "layered down" in the organization. They foresee a loss of status together with a new set of management constraints from above. The hard fact is that frequently it is the good people who jump ship—those critical few who made the company a viable target for acquisition in the first place. These are the people who are the key to its present and future success. Left behind may be little but deadwood, drones, and the disheartened.

Perhaps it should be noted here, too, that bailing out is very contagious. This is primarily because the top talent—key power figures, opinion leaders, and the like—serve as important role models for the rest of the organization. When they jump ship, such action is legitimized. More than that, it popularizes the action. Also, bailouts scare the people who are left behind and make them question the wisdom of remaining themselves. And each bailout represents just one more adjustment for the people who stay, one more point of ambiguity, one more reason to resent the new parent company

So there are many good reasons for trying to identify accurately, and early on, just (1) who it's important to keep, (2) who is likely to leave, and (3) how those important figures can best be induced to stay with the acquisition rather than having them role-model leaving behavior that could be extremely costly.

4

Three Major Sources of Management Turnover

Rule one of *Barron's* 10 Rules for Investors says "The success of a company is dependent nine parts on management and one part on all other factors, including luck."

If that's true for companies in general, it is particularly valid for firms that are being merged or acquired. Toward the end of the conglomerate period of the go-go '60s, Leighton and Tod affirmed this belief in a *Harvard Business Review* article. They wrote,

> We cannot overestimate the importance of getting to know the president and his key personnel. Evidence indicates that the more fully the parent company understands their emotional and personal needs, their weaknesses and strengths, their fears and apprehensions, the more effectively it will be able to help with the acquisition and to manage the company later on.[1]

There are a number of pressing questions that desperately need to be answered:

1. Who should stay?
2. Who should go?
3. Who shall decide, and how?
4. What new managerial demands will a merger bring about?
5. What sort of managerial efficiencies or economies of scale can be achieved?
6. What new management talents will the merger call for—market-realizing savvy, technical expertise, financial acumen, turnaround artistry, team building, a more broad-gauged perspective, fast-growth capability, management of change, etc.?
7. What kind of management potential has been acquired? And what does it imply for long-range personnel planning?
8. How can the newly acquired retinue of managers best be managed and motivated?
9. How does one play to their strengths and shore up their weaknesses?
10. Will the right personal chemistry and compatibility be there? Can I work with these people?

[1] Charles M. Leighton and G. Robert Tod, "After the Acquisition: Continuing Challenge," *Harvard Business Review* 47 (March-April, 1969), p. 94.

The answers to some of these questions, of course, hinge on other issues that must be addressed. Management should establish well-defined criteria by which to evaluate the human resource aspects of the merger. Parent company objectives must be identified as a preliminary step and conclusions drawn regarding how these objectives can best be achieved.

1. To what extent will the organizations be merged?
2. Will the acquisition be run on a centralized basis or be allowed extensive operating autonomy?
3. What control policies and procedures will be implemented to guide the subsidiary?
4. Where operations or functions are overlapping, how will the parent company ascertain which facilities, departments, etc., will be abolished, expanded, or left as they are?

Assuming that the acquiring firm has developed a strategic road map that addresses the integration issues mentioned above, the next order of business would be to make a thorough assessment of ke management and technical talent that initially comes with a new acquisition. And part of this appraisal should be a determination of how much of this talent could be retained.

BAILOUTS

One of the most likely bailout points is seen in the top management ranks. Key executives who fought the merger/acquisition often feel that their relationship with the parent company has been strained beyond repair and that they have too many fences to mend. Feeling that their career is on shaky ground, and without any quick and convincing messages to the contrary from top management in the parent company, they bolt.

The acquirer is frequently taken aback by this turn of events. Parent company executives may believe the relationship is developing quite well and think they have made it plain that they bear no residual ill will. In fact, parent company management sometimes assumes it has done more than is necessary to prevent key managers in the target firm from jumping ship. But assumptions can be extremely costly when dealing with acquisitions, particularly when they lead to vacancies in some of the most critical positions.

Another source of bailouts would be the disgruntled leaders who see themselves being layered away from the top of the power structure so that they suffer a loss of authority or stature. They leave of their own volition because they dislike new reporting relationships that place them further from the top person. Sometimes, though, they jump to conclusions and part company on the basis of false rumors or their own misperceptions. In other instances the acquirer simply fails to do an adequate selling job vis-á-vis how the new organization structure will still offer substantial challenge and, perhaps in the long run, even more career potential. It should be obvious that these bailout candidates will need to have their egos stroked. They need more attention, encouragement, and assurance of their value to the company than they actually get in many instances. The irony is that if they do leave and have to be replaced, the acquirer will end up having to spend much more time and likely quite a bit more money replacing them and bringing the new hires up to speed. Moreover, even when that has been accomplished, the company often has not fully replaced what the departing executives took in terms of technical knowledge, company insights, rapport with the workforce or customers, etc.

Some people turn in their keys and credit cards in the wake of a merger even though their job is secure and they are held in high favor by the parent organization. These departures occur as the incumbents see storm clouds on the horizon regarding new operating styles or management philosophies likely to be imposed by the acquirer.

Here again, some of these people leave on impulse. Taking a fatalistic view of how they will be handled by the new owner, they clear out their desks and leave. Ordinarily they rationalize their behavior as something that grows out of philosophical differences regarding how they feel business should be conducted. But underneath this veneer may be more fundamental psychological forces specifically, a fear of not measuring up, concern about having an inability to meet the new standards, a reluctance to admit that they actually don't know how to do things the parent company way. So again, ego-related issues begin to create merger problems. But the parent company is not likely to hear a key person from the acquired firm say, "Listen, I'm scared. I'm afraid I'm going to look foolish or outclassed." Pride gets in the way, and instead of a cry for help, one hears complaints and criticism aimed at the new owner. So often people pick their words not to reveal who they really are and what they truly think, but rather as a way of concealing fears and protecting themselves. As a result, parent company management commonly fails to perceive the dynamics that are at work. The needed support, encouragement, and coaching are never provided, and the person suffering the insecurities finds an escape route.

Granted, some executives who leave because they do not like the acquirer's operating style or philosophy are extremely confident, secure individuals. They harbor zero concerns about their own ability to measure up. They simply can't accept how the company is supposed to be run in the postmerger setup. At any rate, parent company efforts to keep these people on board should include a concerted communication effort. Pains should be taken to explain the new approach or methodologies—e.g., the justification, the benefits, the specifics regarding how the system will work, and the important role these managers will play in the scheme of things. Naturally some will still leave. But some will stay and adapt well, and both they and the company will benefit.

Some key players jump ship because they cannot (or will not) endure the uncertainty, ambiguity, and stress so characteristic in a new acquisition. Some people can't stand merger politics, so they leave. The best way to hang on to this contingent of employees is to overcome the psychological shockwaves as quickly as possible and then get people oriented toward clear, definitive goals. These people want *closure*. They want to know where they stand, what's expected of them, and whom they will be dealing with in the months to come. The sooner this can be laid out for them, the more likely they are to decide to remain with the firm, settle down, and resume their prior level of productivity

Executives who have been given "golden parachutes" make unusually good bailout material. Likewise, the nouveaux riches who sold their stock and can now walk away with a bundle of money have a new-found freedom. Both sets of people frequently leave the scene simply because they have a variety of reasons for doing so, with only a few weak reasons for staying. Often the parent company bends over backwards to keep these people only to end up with a top-management team that isn't hungry anymore. And as this team's drive and motivation slackens, so does the sense of urgency and the competitive spirit in the rest of the organization.

Finally, there are always people in an acquired firm who seek other job alternatives because they don't like the new corporate direction that, at least in their opinion, the merger portends.   For example, if an employee had plans of building his or her career with a small but growing retail firm and it is taken over by some large, stuffy, bureaucratic organization in a completely different industry, the individual may become a bailout because of the gloomy career future that is foreseen.

It is imperative that the parent company remember, though, that the best people probably find it easiest to leave. Those who possess the most talent will, in all probability, have the greatest number of alternatives, the most promising opportunities dangled before them. These people also will have the most hustle, the most personal initiative, so that they won't wait for opportunity to come knocking. They pursue it. And they are not afraid to seize it even if it means leaving familiar routines and comfortable surroundings.   Certainly they are not averse to leaving the destabilized atmosphere created by a merger.

TERMINATIONS

Insurgents and Obstructionists

In many merger situations, particularly the more adversative takeovers, there are significant people in the acquired firm who refuse to embrace the new order. They are either unwilling or unable to adapt to the new scheme of things. These people pose a problem on two counts. First, at a time when the organization needs facilitative influences, they are an obstruction. They get in the way of the needed changes, whether as a result of personal rigidity, lack of competence, or simply rebellion against the new owner. Second, they tend to become somewhat insurgent, infecting others with their negativism and resistance to change. Typically they rationalize away their own inadequacies and project blame onto the parent company, accusing it of being responsible for the shortcomings in their job performance. They fan the flames of unrest, sometimes subtly and surreptitiously, sometimes blatantly. Particularly when in positions of authority or high visibility, they easily provoke greater discontent among other personnel.

Sometimes, of course, this undesirable behavior can be eliminated if the parent company (1) gets an accurate fix on who these people are and (2) confronts the problem head-on. But while some individuals have within themselves the ability and the willingness to change their attitudes and upgrade their work behavior, others never do.

Those people who do not succeed in getting on board should be separated from the organization. When they are indulged, allowed second or third chances, or merely given a light slap on the wrist, the parent company is essentially reinforcing the wrong behavior. Much better for the acquirer to set definite limits, communicate those in a clear and distinct fashion, and then enforce them firmly. This can send an important, unmistakable message to bystanders in the acquired firm who are watching attentively to see how the new management deals with personnel problems. Not only is it important for the success of the merger that the insurgents be terminated, it is also essential that the early precedents be designed to communicate clearly the new rules or standards by which top management plans to operate.

Executives in the acquiring firm lose credibility and respect when they drag their feet in making needed terminations. Management can be firm without being ruthless and equitable without being indulgent. Such an approach is in the long-run best interest of both the organization and the employee.

Staffing Duplications

The merging of two organizations routinely creates superfluous or excess personnel as a result of the consolidation of departments, integration of functions, or elimination of certain work groups. When two companies with duplicate functions merge, obviously there are redundancies that cannot be justified from a payroll standpoint.

Further, mergers are frequently sought for the economies of scale they permit, and this means that in all likelihood some people will need to be dismissed.

Ordinarily when such reorganizations are contemplated, the parent company should move expeditiously to make the realignments and complete the merger process. To begin with, people can usually sense when such an integration of firms is likely, and organizational momentum suffers badly until that process has been finalized. The more quickly top management moves in, making its restructuring and staffing decisions, the more it gets to exercise its preferred options. In the early stages, the best performers are still in the picture and therefore can more likely be given key assignments sufficiently challenging to keep them with the company. On the other hand, if the reorganization and reassignments come too slowly, the acquisition frequently stalls out and good people go elsewhere to seek their fortunes.

Nonperformers

When the acquisition of a firm is carried out as a financial salvage operation, there typically is strong logic arguing in favor of replacing some of the key people. The executives who carried the organization into red ink and who are seen as part of the problem instead of the solution are obvious candidates for termination. To leave these executives at the helm may run the risk of sabotaging any turnaround effort attempted by the acquirer. The tough question, and one that deserves a well-researched answer, is "Which incumbents should be retained for the contribution they could make to the ailing firm's rehabilitation?"

Even those acquired firms that are financially sturdy will often have selected personnel who, for one reason or another, are not performing up to par. Perhaps they were indulged by the company for one reason or another, managed to escape notice somehow, or led a charmed life that allowed them to survive without really earning their keep. Under the more scrutinizing, nonpartisan eye of management in the new parent company, however, these people will be found wanting and should be encouraged to leave.

There are several good reasons for moving promptly to separate these employees. First, if they are not contributing that much, better to let them go and remove that drain on the payroll. Second, this action communicates a worthwhile message to others throughout the acquisition to the effect that the new owner has little tolerance for nonperformance. This sort of termination gets the word across that mediocrity can be a risk to job security. A third argument supporting the idea of expeditiously terminating weak people is that such action generally is applauded by those in the acquired firm who are good performers. The capable people, those who are really productive ordinarily will have grown quite weary of having to carry the load that should have been borne by others.

Thus, when the new owner steps forth purposefully to purge the acquired firm of weak people, he customarily meets with the approval of the real contributors. In fact, this should serve as a motivating event for contributors and is related to the fourth reason for expeditiously terminating the incumbents who haven't been measuring up as they should. Specifically, when lackluster performers are let go, that opens up slots which allow the promotion and reassignment of more promising personnel. This kind of housecleaning and reallocation of human resources is particularly appropriate in the merger/acquisition arena where people are expecting change.

Opportunities for Streamlining

Top management in the acquiring firm usually finds that just as there is a need to get rid of insurgents, redundant personnel, and nonperformers, there is also some fat that can be trimmed. Practically all organizations accrue a certain amount of excess baggage as years go by. It's an insidious process, and something to which the target company grows accustomed, but the sharp eye of the acquirer should be able to ascertain where these opportunities for streamlining exist.

There may be people in the management ranks who are a manifestation of the Peter Principle—i.e., people who have "reached their level of incompetence" and are quite expendable. Perhaps in being kicked upstairs they have been made relatively harmless, but if they are in over their heads, and particularly if they are rather nonproductive, they should be viewed as candidates for termination. Again, the vacancies created may provide superb opportunities to promote up-and-comers who can revitalize the acquired firm.

There may be others on board who, though quite capable and even reasonably productive, have been given makeshift assignments that fall short of justifying their continuing existence on the company roster. Some of these folks may be worthy of reassignment or transfer, but at the very least their work role should be scrutinized and their contribution carefully weighed. If these people cannot be channeled along more productive paths then they, too, should be dismissed.

Other incumbents may be identified who have ended up in assignments for which they are poorly cast. The postmerger environment can be an opportune time to correct these unsuitable appointments that have been tolerated too long. Some of these mismatches may indeed involve high-caliber talent that could be most beneficial to the acquired (or parent) firm if the people were reassigned. But this calls for careful assessment of both the person and the organizational needs, an appraisal process that should occur early in the postmerger scheme of things. If it is determined that these personnel are expendable, then in all likelihood the ties should be severed as part of a global, systematic effort to make the acquired firm more lean and trim.

PEOPLE RECRUITED AWAY FROM THE FIRM

When word begins to circulate that a company has been targeted for acquisition, it often pricks up the ears of corporate recruiters and executive search consultants. They know, at least implicitly, that the event will increase the likelihood that people within the firm to be acquired will be more approachable than before. The situation is viewed as "open season," one of the easiest times to lure away technical specialists, key managers, and executives.

Mergers and acquisitions generally cause people to reassess their careers, examine their alternatives, and check out promising options.

In other words, they become much more amenable to putting themselves on the market, whereas under normal circumstances they might prefer to remain settled, steadfast, and secure in their jobs. These employees may not have looked at the employment ads for many years. Ordinarily they might be inclined to dismiss any overtures another potential employer might send their way. But being acquired changes all that.

High-talent people, in particular, will often opt for immediate guarantees they can negotiate with a new employer rather than wait out the merger situation and gamble that their careers will be well served (or at least not damaged) by the acquisition of their firm. This is especially true when the parent organization has a bad reputation in the business world for its handling of acquisitions.

Those who are recruited away might never have become bailouts, much less terminations, but they still can become a part of management turnover statistics. When they leave, ordinarily they not only weaken the company but also frequently end up strengthening the competition that has stepped in to take advantage of the situation.

5

The Need for a Comprehensive Appraisal of the Acquired Company's Management Resources

Over the years, the conventional practice of making staffing changes on the heels of an acquisition has taken one of two different forms. Sometimes the acquired firm steps in early to make people changes, whether in just a handful of positions or with wholesale reorganization. In the other approach, the parent company attempts to maintain a hands-off stance—again, except for perhaps one or two initial changes—until several months have elapsed that hopefully allow enough time for everybody to calm down and become adjusted to the situation. One of the familiar steps in this second tactic involves assurances from executives in the parent company to the effect that "We don't plan any personnel changes."

In both of these approaches, however, the critical thing that's missing is a systematic, incisive assessment of what the acquisition brings vis-á-vis management and technical talent. Occasionally, although it is remarkably rare, an acquiring firm will take a piecemeal approach wherein a few people here and there are evaluated in a professional fashion. Or a number of people may be appraised in a sketchy manner, but so superficially that much room remains for potential problems to develop.

Top management in the acquiring firm might argue that it is best to allow some time for them to get to know the abilities and potentials of the management team in the target organization. But that assumes that those people will hang around long enough for such a familiarization process to occur. Often they do not. Furthermore, while taking the slow route, a part of this getting-acquainted exercise may consist of seeing bad management decisions being made, mistakes that could have been prevented. Likewise, key opportunities may be lost. All in all this can prove to be an expensive and time-consuming education process. This approach also drags out the integration of the two firms. It forestalls needed resolution and leaves questions unanswered, prolonging the anxiety and ambiguity, thus contributing to the chronic problem of post-merger drift.

This approach is not necessarily a kind and thoughtful way of dealing with staffing matters. Nor is it likely to be viewed favorably by people in the acquired organization. Rather than looking on this as a fair and equitable opportunity to prove themselves, they will more likely be anxiously waiting to see when and where the axe will fall.

The situation may feel like benign neglect to people in the acquisition, as if they are being left to dangle helplessly in the wind. In their opinion, it probably would be better to get closure, to be appraised promptly and fairly, so that they can get on with their careers either secure in the merged firm or somewhere else.

WHY NOT "DANCE WITH THEM THAT BRUNG YOU?"

It might be argued that in several merger scenarios it is best to go with the status quo.   That is, move on the premise that the incumbent management team is sound and the acquiring company should not fool around with something that's working.   That line of reasoning sounds good on the surface, especially if the acquired firm is financially healthy and has a pretty good track record.   Upon careful scrutiny, however, it proves to be flawed in a number of respects.

Some people won't stay and dance. To begin with, the acquirer needs to ascertain who is *willing* to stay. The new owner may be extremely fond of the new charges and fully confident that they can continue to operate their company in a successful fashion.   But that's no guarantee whatsoever that the feelings are reciprocal.   Even if these incumbents are not grumbling, even if they appear to be reconciled to the situation, in-depth data gathering often proves otherwise.   The acquirer should consider it essential to rapidly identify fast-track, high-talent employees so that the parent company can put forth special efforts to retain them.   Often these people can be "hooked" with heavy-duty assignments and special developmental opportunities which clearly communicate the key role they can play in the organization's future.

It is particularly important for the new owner to take pains to identify these people and tie them to the organization if the acquisition represents a move by the parent company into new terrain—e.g., unfamiliar products/services, different markets, etc.   The less one understands the business that has been bought, the more crucial it is to keep those people on board who do have a firm grasp of what it takes to make the business a success.   The same general idea holds true, of course, if the acquirer does not have any surplus management talent to speak of that could be sent across to manage things in the event key vacancies develop in the acquisition. And after an adversative merger battle has been fought, as in a raid or contested situation, the question of who is willing to stay is a particularly sensitive issue.

Some people don't dance very well. Virtually any management team has a weak link here or there. And the odds are that even a successful company can work better if the weaker performers are identified. This does not mean that they will always be replaced. But parent company executives can determine how best to maneuver around a person's shortcomings by compensating for them through the use of support personnel, changing certain features of the job itself, or focusing on developing the incumbent's skills. At any rate, the parent company can be well served by early identification of management vulnerabilities. It can preempt many nasty, costly surprises by giving the parent firm an opportunity to take preventive measures.

Also, if the merger has brought about departmental overlap or duplicated functions, and the integration game plan calls for keeping only one person in those situations, an early evaluation will indicate which person should be groomed to fill the one opening that will remain.

Data for management succession planning. The acquirer needs to know where promotion potential exists in order that good management succession planning can take place. There is virtually always some early turnover in key management positions, and decisions must be made regarding promotions, transfers, and recruitment of new blood. A broad-gauged management assessment develops the kind of database necessary to move decisively in those situations.

Executives in the parent company can benefit from having an accurate "fix" on people's limits plus their potential for shouldering heavier duties or altogether different types of assignments. The merger/acquisition arena is no place for trial-and-error staffing decisions.

Learn how to manage and motivate. By getting a quick, comprehensive set of insights into the makeup of the management corps in the acquired company, the parent firm possesses the information needed to best manage and motivate these people from day one.

Ordinarily, it will be found that some of the acquired personnel need generous job structure—that is, clear-cut marching orders, very specific objectives, and definitive procedural guidelines. Others will be found who operate best in an environment where they are given very free rein and generous latitude to exercise their own judgment. Some people are best motivated by attention, approval, and hand-holding, although others will perform best under a strict boss who is quick to discipline.

The key point here is that it is very easy to mismanage, and there-in demotivate, people whom you don't know. It is extremely easy to violate the practices people have grown accustomed to over the years. When that happens, the odds are significantly increased that bailouts will occur, that people will be recruited away more easily, or at least that their job performance will deteriorate.

Identify training needs. Some people—even some of the best talent—need additional training to measure up to the new demands they will encounter as they struggle to adapt to new operating styles and the like.

Keep in mind that it is just as likely as not that these people will prefer to keep quiet about the struggle they are having. They will be highly unaccustomed to asking for help. This suggests, then, that the acquirer needs to be highly sensitive to where incumbent personnel will in all likelihood need training or coaching.

Opportunity for coaching and management development. Since mergers and acquisitions produce so much dissonance, since they are such a destabilizing force, they typically act as an "unfreezing" event for employees. People are jarred out of their familiar routines. There is a significant increase in introspection, leading managers and others to examine themselves and their modus operandi. This mental state makes them far more receptive to the idea of behavior change or efforts aimed toward self-improvement.

Thus, on the heels of an acquisition, the timing is right for management development activities.

A careful, thorough evaluation in this atmosphere produces data that can be shared with an incumbent in a very meaningful feedback session.   With receptivity to personal change being at a peak, constructive coaching is far more likely to produce desired behavior change than it would in ordinary circumstances.

Assessing adaptability.   Some people who did well under the old regime will not be able to adapt to the new setup.   For example, the new system may not tolerate or indulge their shortcomings and idiosyncrasies.

The company may be moving out of a fast-growth mode into a stabilization period, and this may call for more of a "maintenance manager." Or it may be that in the months ahead the company will need high-powered marketing savvy more than the financial expertise an incumbent has.   A person who did well in a more structured, premerger environment may now be surpassed by someone who fared poorly in that world but has the capacity to shine in the current climate of ambiguity.

At any rate, a professionally conducted appraisal may well identify which people are likely to become weak performers, passive resisters, or even clear-cut insurgents.   It is ironic that usually some of the best people in the acquired company adapt most slowly to the postmerger requirements.   This seems to occur because strong performers typically are very committed to their own style and pursue their own priorities with such conviction.

Search for new talents.   A merger may mean that new, previously unimportant skills and abilities are crucial to the future success of the company.   What worked before may now be obsolete or at least not enough.

In planning for the future, parent companies should not generalize too freely from the past.   John Kitching, reporting on a Harvard study in an article titled "Why Mergers Miscarry," emphasizes that the critical element for success "is the existence or absence of 'managers of change'—men who can catalyze the combination process," adding "In the most successful mergers, either the acquiring company brought in new managers of change or it motivated the old management to introduce profitable change."[1]

Measuring motivation.   Executives, previously highly driven performers, may lose much of their motivation if the merger makes them independently wealthy.   Their commitment may drop with a resulting sag in their day-to-day performance.   Entrepreneurial spirit, initiative, and resourcefulness frequently deteriorate in key players once they are cloaked in financial security.   There are also other merger dynamics at work to compound the problem—e.g., loss of clear role identity, the fact that ultimate fiscal responsibility rests with someone else, less feeling of ownership, a drop in independent authority, and so on.

The owner/entrepreneur, in particular, is prone to feel rather inhibited if he or she remains to operate in the postmerger setting. People such as this are not accustomed to having to answer to anyone. Now, with skilled and rather sophisticated executives there to second-guess and require adherence to a new management style and unfamiliar performance measures, the owner/entrepreneur often becomes anxious.   There is an overwhelming fear of being seen as inept. Those who are not insecure may become demotivated out of aggravation.   An in-house merger/acquisition paper at Westinghouse submits that,

> Few owner/managers are, in fact, worth to the business what it would take to fully motivate them toward long-term, high-level performance on behalf of "their" business. A higher percentage of Westinghouse acquisitions should be accompanied by the planned replacement of top management of the acquired company either immediately or after a short transition period.

So a thorough assessment is serviceable here in two respects— first, in anticipating which personnel are likely to slacken off and, second, in providing the parent company with insight into the trials facing the owner/entrepreneur. The essential point is that incumbents cannot be adequately evaluated strictly on the basis of history or past performance.   Rather, they must be measured against the future in terms of what it brings by way of goals to be accomplished and problems to be overcome.

---

[1]John Kitching, "Why Mergers Miscarry," *Harvard Business Review XLV* (November-December, 1967), p. 91.

What really accounts for the company's track record? The company's past success may be due primarily to factors other than abilities and efforts of incumbent management. A broad-gauged management assessment can give valuable clues regarding this sort of situation.

The same thing is true, of course, in the other direction. A firm that is courting bankruptcy is not always devoid of competent managers and executives. There may well be bona fide winners in the crowd somewhere and, if so, they should prove to be most valuable helping the acquirer effect a turnaround if they are identified and retained.

A database to aid in corporate integration. Finally, there is value in conducting a thoroughgoing assessment of the management group simply for the database it can generate for use in team-building activities that, ideally, should be a part of the merger integration process.

WHY NOT EVALUATE THE ACQUIRED COMPANY'S MANAGEMENT ON THE BASIS OF CORPORATE GROWTH AND PROFITABILITY?

This is the most traditional approach, and it is good so far as that goes. Certainly, it does pay respect to salient—even critical—data.

But as Dave Dreman wrote in *Forbes*, "Most of us consider companies well managed when sales, earnings, and, most importantly, stock prices are moving ahead rapidly; badly managed when they aren't." Dreman goes on to share some research results from *Perspectives*, an institutional investor publication of Steve Leuthold:

> According to Leuthold, there is a fairly widespread consensus among many brokerage houses and financial publications as to which are the best-managed companies. In fact, numbers of them put out their annual selections. *Perspectives* analyzed one such list in which a magazine provided five choices yearly between 1972 and 1980. The study measured the performance of each pick from the time it was placed on the list to the end of 1981. In all, 45 companies were placed in the "Best Managed" category.

> The bottom line: "At year-end 1981 our 'Buy-the-Best Management' investor had a portfolio that appreciated only 19 percent compared with the appreciation of 37 percent for the S&P 500," says Leuthold. The S&P had outperformed the best-managed companies by a factor of almost two to one. Further, since the best-managed companies paid much lower dividends than the S&P, if dividend reinvesting was included (as is normal in calculating overall returns), the comparison against the S&P would have worsened considerably.[2]

The key point here is that good numbers still can mask weak talent. The acquired company may for all practical purposes have been a one-man show. There may be no backup. That in itself is bad enough, but it becomes even more critical if the front man happens to depart in the aftermath of the acquisition.

There are simply too many external biasing factors that deserve consideration for the parent company to simply assume that incumbents truly do deserve full credit for the current set of numbers. A quantitative analysis can be misleading in a variety of ways.

A product of good times. A benevolent economy may deserve most of the credit for the acquired firm's good financial performance. And as Dave Dreman explained in 1982, "The business outlook can change substantially, so that a 1978 winner like Caterpillar or a 1980 winner like American-Standard is merely treading water today."[3] So the question that deserves thought is whether there is much proof that incumbents can manage a down economy or a postmerger situation successfully.

Short-term perspective. Management may be guilty of mortgaging the future to achieve short-term results. Statistics that look good today may have been achieved at tomorrow's expense.

For example, the financial ledger may look good because there has been no money spent on R&D, capital improvements, etc. The work force may have been slashed to cut overhead, but this may have been done at the expense of adequate servicing of the company's

---

[2]David Dreman, "What Is Best Managed," *Forbes* 129 (March 15, 1982), p. 168.

[3]Dreman, "What Is Best Managed," p. 168.

products. And given time, these sorts of executive decisions could conceivably prove to be devastating to the firm. Numbers that good on the surface may actually be fragile evidence of executive talent. Management may have built a house of cards that faces a very shaky, uncertain future.

The hand of fate. Pure luck may have been on the company's side. Chance timing may deserve most of the credit, as management simply may have stumbled into good fortune. Or a foolish gamble may have worked, although it never should have been taken.

The trend that has buoyed the financial picture may be about to reverse—e.g., a fast-growth strategy may be on the brink of corporate wreckage as financial resources are overextended and management capacities strained beyond reason.

Who really deserves the credit? It is possible that good numbers result primarily from the backup strength given by managers or technically skilled individuals who have already left the firm or who probably will leave. Likewise, managers or technical people may have been in slots where their own effectiveness has been masked by the strong or weak performance of another person.

In other words, who really owns the statistics? Who is primarily responsible for the acquired firm's present financial status? Who has taken up the slack for whom?

A race with only one runner. A quantitatively favorable picture may be the result of little or no competition. And that, of course, can conceivably change.

So long as one has the only grocery store in town, the numbers may look pretty good, but they may say very little about managerial competence. It is interesting to observe how many major corporations have appeared to be well managed until they were confronted with stiff competition from Japanese imports in the form of automobiles, steel, and electronics.

Environmental forces. Changing markets and changing access to raw materials due to political/governmental forces may cause top management to have numbers that look particularly good or bad. For example, Japan's steel dumping practices, the OPEC oil cartel, import tariffs, and price supports exemplify external forces that can bias a company's financial picture dramatically without making any valid statement about the caliber of the management team.

False statistics. Numbers often lie. And they are often manipulated to make top management look better than it should.

For example, the way inventories and facilities are valued, the tax angles that are played, and other accounting shenanigans can present a very misleading picture regarding top management's true track record.

In his book *How to Measure Managerial Performance,* Richard Sloma states:

> Output from the accounting system, while perfectly acceptable to the public audit firm, may be not only useless to a management performance measurement program, but actually counterproductive, in that management performance may be inaccurately measured. The "best" array of measures always includes a "blend" of data, from both outside and within the accounting system.[4]

How versus how much. Qualitative issues or factors may be more important than quantitative measures. For instance, an executive's ethics, strategic vision, human relations skills, etc., may deserve more consideration than the numbers he can boast. Perhaps he swung a $50 million deal by making a $50,000 bribe. Possibly he achieved impressive market share by stealing trade secrets. It might be that the CEO has an adversative manner that has enabled him or her to aggressively generate some good financial results thus far, but that will eventually precipitate a strike or lawsuit.

In short, you can't separate the ends from the means. Bernie Cornfeld was viewed as a high-powered, go-go executive until his Investors Overseas Services cratered and he took the money and ran.

There were plenty of small and medium-sized oil companies with

---

[4]Richard S. Sloma, *How To Measure Managerial Performance* (New York. Macmillan, 1980), p.3

mediocre, even weak management teams that were blazing financial successes during 1980. The numbers were there, but strong management talent was not. And there were dynamic, highly capable managers and executives being ground into the dirt by the financial woes of such mainstream industries as steel, autos, and home construction. To gauge the latter group's ability and potential on the basis of their miserable corporate statements would have been at best misleading and essentially ridiculous. But all too often the leaders of an acquired firm are appraised on the basis of quantitative data—the profits or the bottom line, what the company has shown vis-á-vis earnings, stock prices, and growth in revenues. Parent company executives need to scrutinize the *qualitative* data on its acquired management team, as this information represents part of the "hidden economics" of the deal.

WHAT'S WRONG WITH LETTING INCUMBENT EXECU-TIVES IN THE TARGET COMPANY SUBMIT AN APPRAISAL OF ITS OWN MANAGEMENT TEAM?

Take what the president, CEO, or owner has to offer, but don't take for granted that the acquired firm can give you an accurate, unbiased appraisal of its own incumbent managers. The people mentioned may not be able to and may not want to. Usually the data they supply can be extremely helpful, but they are far from being a sufficiently thorough, reliable critique.

Usually the top-ranking individual gives an off-the-cuff evaluation of key people in the firm, if there is a critique given at all. On one hand, it's astounding that acquirers are no more consistent than they are in using this person as a source for these data. But then it is also amazing that some acquirers are so ready to take at face value what this person might say about subordinates.

There are myriad reasons for questioning the validity and completeness of this person's critique of management and other personnel in the acquisition. Imagine a situation in which the man involved in negotiating the sale of a company has been asked by the acquirer to evaluate some of his key people.

Parting gestures. This may be the senior executive's best (perhaps last) chance to repay old debts to incumbents. Thus, it is almost certain that he will feel certain obligations to defend them. If the owner has sold the organization and plans to leave the picture, he will want to be remembered fondly. He may also suffer pangs of guilt as a result of having sold the company, and in attempting to assuage these feelings, may allow a positive bias to creep into the management critique.

The last to know. It is not uncommon to find that the owner or CEO is actually somewhat out of touch with his people and their plans. It might be, for example, that a couple of key executives are on the verge of leaving to start a competing firm. The top executive almost always fails to maintain quite as accurate a feel for the pulse of the organization when much of his time and energies are directed toward finding a buyer, negotiating a sale, or perhaps trying to fend off a corporate raider.

Promoting the in-crowd. Where the key executive plans to remain in an active role with the firm, he may strive—even unconsciously—to entrench his loyalists and thereby retain a power base of his own. It is extremely difficult to be objective, and not be protective, of one's own advocates or constituency.

Wrong perspective. The acquired company's top executive may not really grasp what the firm will need by way of management talent in the postmerger situation. He may not know where the buyer plans to go with the new acquisition. Unless he is really on the right wavelength, his appraisal of subordinates vis-á-vis the new corporate future will be unreliable.

Blind spots. The owner or key executive in the acquired firm simply may not be a very good judge of talent and ability. He may attribute success to the wrong people, such as lauding the vice president of sales for the firm's revenues instead of crediting some outstanding sales managers who actually managed to achieve the excellent sales volumes in spite of the vice president of sales. It is common to find top executives overrating certain traits or factors while underrating the importance of others. For example, a man who doesn't like subordinates that challenge him will often view aggressiveness as a negative attribute when it might be a highly sought characteristic by management in the parent organization.

Pride of ownership. There is a vested interest on the part of the senior executive as he proceeds to critique the strengths and weaknesses of subordinates. After all, he is responsible for putting this team together in the first place. It's his handiwork. He is very much ego-involved. In evaluating the management team negatively, he would essentially be criticizing himself and his own performance. It is very difficult to do that without pulling punches.

Blackball. It may be that a person in the acquired company with real talent has been blacklisted along the way somehow, and thus may not be evaluated justly by superiors.

No bearer of bad news. The acquired company's top officer may say what he thinks you want to hear instead of laying cold, hard, and unwelcome facts on the line.

Remember, if this is the company that the owner or CEO has been trying to sell, undoubtedly he has been presenting it in the most favorable light. He has probably been singing its praises—highlighting its good points—while downplaying, ignoring, or even concealing its flaws and vulnerable features. It could take months to find out just how weak some acquired managers are, and by then the damage is usually already done: opportunities have been lost, accounts have been bungled, etc.

Familiar words, different meanings. The key executive in the acquisition probably does not know the parent company well enough to evaluate people from that frame of reference. Parent company norms may be quite different regarding what is seen as good, what is mediocre, and what is weak.

The standards and the semantics can vary dramatically from one company to another, particularly if they are in different industries and are of widely divergent sizes.

Charges of bias from people in the acquiring firm. People in the parent company may not accept the critique as a fair, objective appraisal. Moreover, they probably shouldn't for the very reasons mentioned above. The more there is to be a true merger of the two organizations, the more this becomes a problem of real significance. If managers or technical personnel from the two companies will be vying for the same slots, a more objective, nonpartisan means of appraising candidates needs to be arranged.

Who's outside the inner circle? People inside the acquired company may wish for an external, objective evaluation that precludes cronyism, nepotism, or other means of playing favorites. Even if the parent company did happen to be comfortable with the idea that the acquisition's owner or CEO can provide an adequate and equitable appraisal of incumbent managers, some of the people working for him may not be comfortable with the idea at all. Furthermore, they may have very good reasons for feeling that way.

Will history repeat itself? Finally, it could well be that some incumbents in the acquired firm will do things (or have done things) for the "old man" they would never do for the parent company— e. g., make personal sacrifices or exhibit unusual commitment. The very same people, under the new parent company's influence and management, may give an altogether different performance. It may be worse, it may be even better. Either way, the "old man's" appraisal of these people may be a very accurate description of what he has experienced in the relationship, but it may not be duplicated under the new regime.

WHAT'S WRONG WITH HAVING SOME EXECUTIVES IN THE ACQUIRING COMPANY MAKE A CASUAL, SUBTLE, INFORMAL ASSESSMENT OF THE TARGET COMPANY'S MANAGEMENT TEAM?

Again, nothing is wrong so long as this approach is not over-rated. This can provide a particularly important assessment on some technical matters and "personal chemistry" issues.

Still, there are a variety of problems in relying on this means of determining the strengths and weaknesses of the acquired firm's human resources.

Questionable objectivity. Some of the executives in the parent company may have something to lose. They may have an axe to grind so that they cannot be sufficiently objective. Often this is an unconscious bias, but very pernicious just the same.

It is conceivable that a particularly high-powered, ambitious individual in the target company poses a bit of a threat, e.g., if one of the acquirer's executives envisions the possibility that they could both be vying for the same position some day in the not too distant future. Or perhaps the parent company executive has been mentoring somebody in his own organization who must now compete with this talented newcomer.

Sometimes the bias grows out of the unstated assumption that "We're the buyer, that must mean we're better." This mental syndrome frequently pervades the parent company, adds to the polarization of the two firms, and contributes to unfair comparisons of people.

Evaluate the evaluator. So much of the time this sort of appraisal exercise does not play to the strengths of the parent company executives who are involved in the process. They may give it their best shot, and even do a respectable job, but the odds are it does not represent their real forte. This evaluation remains a crucial task, however, and should be conducted in as professional a manner as possible.

Shooting from the hip. A casual, informal evaluation is just not sufficient. Too much is at stake to take a haphazard, unsystematic approach to appraising the competencies of key people in the acquired firm. But the evaluation is almost always an unstructured exercise when it is being done by parent company executives. Ordinarily these executives sort of play it by ear, leaning much too heavily on "gut feel," inconsistent measures, and incomplete data.

Other priorities. Usually parent company executives have their hands full doing other things. For them to become heavily involved in this appraisal process pulls them away from tasks where their best abilities likely can be better employed. And the very fact that they are busy and preoccupied with other priorities increases the odds that this task will be shortchanged in terms of the time and effort it receives.

Lowering the trust level. If it is very apparent that, in fact, they are being evaluated by the parent company, the incumbents in the acquisition will probably be more guarded and defensive than they would if they were being evaluated by an outsider. The people under consideration are far more likely to open up and share feelings and perceptions if the evaluation is conducted by someone who can bring objectivity as well as professionalism to the task. Furthermore, incumbents are almost certain to view this evaluation as a more fair and equitable assessment of their abilities and potential.

WHAT'S WRONG WITH CLEANING HOUSE?

Sometimes the acquirer elects to make wholesale changes. Rather than go through the exercise of having anyone do much of an assessment of incumbents, they are unilaterally dismissed and—in those positions deemed necessary for continued company operations—replaced with new recruits or with transfers from the parent company.

This may appear to be the line of least resistance, but that appearance probably is deceiving. Even when an acquisition involves rescuing a company from insolvency, there is a more prudent way to deal with staffing decisions and management succession planning. The problems are manifold in deciding to clean house.

Salvage what you can. Housecleaning probably means throwing out the good with the bad. Somewhere in the management ranks there is bound to be some valuable talent that should be retained.

Bridging the gap. Housecleaning sacrifices people who possess a valuable sense of history regarding the company and who can give your corporate effort an important element of continuity. In their absence, the transition period is likely to be significantly prolonged.

The parent company invariably will find that the acquired firm suffers a severe loss of momentum during the restaffing process. The postmerger dip in productivity is almost always an inescapable problem, but while it cannot be avoided completely, it certainly can be minimalized. It is compounded, however, when there is a broad-ranging purge of existing personnel.

Intangible assets. The acquirer loses whatever is "in people's heads" regarding operations, products, the competition, etc. In virtually any organization there are undeveloped ideas and programs that have substantial value, but which have not been put in writing or another form of permanent record. Important data regarding how business is conducted have not been captured in any book of procedures or operating guidelines. Incumbents succeed in dealing with certain clients because of the intimate insights that have been developed over time, but this is carried with them when they leave. These intangibles can never be fully retrieved.

Polarization. Cleaning house threatens and alienates the remaining work force, fostering a highly adversarial climate. Furthermore, because of the extremely adverse impact it has on trust level, behavior is driven underground and the communication networks take a long time to recover. Overall, the event has a strong inhibiting influence on those employees who remain. At the very time the acquirer needs the most from these people, they become much more cautious and self-protective as they go about their duties.

Damaged business relationships. As part of the housecleaning, the parent company risks the loss of key contacts that have been developed over the years. The ties that have been forged with political and civic leaders, customers, or even suppliers are commonly based on personal friendships. These important outsiders are often offended by the way their friends have been treated by the new owner and therefore seek their own vengeance. Key accounts may go elsewhere and it may become much more difficult to negotiate with vendors. Power brokers in the business community or the government sector can create innumerable obstacles that otherwise would never have developed.

Wasted efforts. This approach ordinarily derails valuable projects or programs that are in progress, but that are not far enough along to survive on their own. This could include research efforts, marketing plans, new product development, and training or other personnel programs.

Demotivation. Wholesale terminations are usually devastating to morale in the acquired firm as the employees see their organization being dismembered. Job commitment and company loyalty fizzle. Thus, intangible motivating forces that may have been important components of the firm's previous success no longer exist. Key facets of the underlying corporate culture are dislodged, resulting in a more apathetic work force that is unresponsive to the new owner's attempts to rally and regroup those employees who remain.

Stiffening the opposition. This approach chases incumbents over to the competitor's house, where their knowledge can really be damaging to the parent company. Not only do they take their talents to the opposition, they go with a vindictive spirit. So the acquirer ends up with new enemies both within and without.

A troublesome reputation. Housecleaning gives rise to an image of the parent company as a ruthless acquirer. Obviously this label can plague the new owner later on in any subsequent acquisition efforts. Most companies are very leery of talking merger with a firm that has developed this kind of reputation. Even when subsequent deals are struck and the acquirer has no intention of being "the new broom that sweeps clean," people in the target firm will be running scared because of the parent company's notoriety.

A dollar drain. If some of the incumbent managers or executives have arranged golden parachutes for themselves, housecleaning can become a very costly approach from a purely monetary standpoint. Finally, restating can become an expensive exercise in and of itself. Executives' time spent in courting, interviewing, and orienting replacement personnel adds up in a hurry.

Wrap-up points. To sum it up, then, there are several admonitions for consideration by the parent company.

First, the new owner should not be tempted to "go with the familiar person." This tactic does not sufficiently minimize the risks that are involved.

Second, there is real danger in adhering to the conventional wisdom which says, "Do nothing and wait for the dust to settle." It may, on the surface, appear that in employing this approach one is exercising sage restraint. But once the dust has settled, some good people may well be gone. Some will have been waffling along with a wait-and-see attitude. Still others will have done damage that could have been prevented by a more timely termination or reassignment. Undoubtedly the organization will have lost some momentum unnecessarily while also wasting an excellent opportunity to motivate people.

Third, sweeping personnel changes that follow closely on the heels of an acquisition, and which proceed without any systematic appraisal of those people being terminated, come at too dear a cost.

6

A Three-Way Evaluation of Managerial and Technical Talent

A systematic appraisal of significant personnel in an acquisition calls for input from several directions. A multifaceted approach generates a database that is most useful because it is (1) more accurate and (2) more informative than any appraisal growing out of a single data source.

The first and most obvious appraisal of incumbents should draw on the insights of the owner and/or senior executive in the acquired firm. The second stage in the three-way process should be an objective, professional evaluation conducted by a management/ organizational psychologist. The third data input should consist of the perceptions of executives in the acquiring organization. When the three sets of data are blended, a very serviceable composite picture should emerge of each one of the key people in the acquired firm.

INPUT FROM THE ACQUIRED FIRM'S OWNER OR CEO

The dangers of relying too heavily on this data input have already been highlighted. Nevertheless, it does remain a logical point of inquiry vis-á-vis the abilities, potentials, attitudes, and orientations of incumbents.

What is needed, and what is usually not employed, is a systematic and consistent format for this senior executive to follow in sharing his or her thoughts about subordinates. Ideally it will take the form of a structured interview conducted by another person—e.g., a management/organizational psychologist or perhaps a senior manager in the parent company's personnel department. This third party conducts the interview, adhering to the structured format and thus ensuring that all incumbents are appraised with the same level of thoroughness and according to the same sort of rating criteria.

Invariably there is a fund of rich data in the key executive's head if this third party can just elicit, organize, and interpret it appropriately. The owner or CEO is in a position to evaluate subordinates in the context of the company he or she knows better than anyone else does. This person probably has the best grasp of make-or-break traits and talents, too, such that incumbents are appraised on highly relevant behavior or characteristics. Ordinarily, this senior executive can readily cite a number of "critical incidents" that substantiate the assessment.

The third party conducting the interview plays another key role in helping the senior executive past his or her own personal biases or halo effects. This permits the pros and cons to be weighed more dispassionately

A side benefit of these interviews is that the third party will invariably glean critically valuable insights into the acquired firm's organizational culture or personality, operating style, predominant managerial philosophy, and overall company norms. These insights can be most valuable in subsequent efforts to facilitate integration of the two companies.

The third party should have the top executive critique the key managers and technical specialists by structuring an analysis of these incumbents individually on the following points:

- Major strengths.
- Weaker points or shortcomings.
- How this person compensates, or what accounts most for his or her job effectiveness.
- Record of achieving goals and objectives.
- Major accomplishments/contributions.
- Major mistakes/problems in past performance.
- Management style.
- Most common management mistakes.
- Environment in which the person works best (and worst).
- Transferability to other job assignments or management responsibilities.
- Where the person needs backup and support.
- Problems in managing the individual.
- How the person can best be motivated.
- Next logical career step.
- Long-range potential.
- Developmental needs.

Having accomplished that, the third party then should pursue a line of questioning designed to get a better feel for how the employee is likely to react to the merger/acquisition. Here the inquiry should address such topics as the following:

- How the person will react to the merger/acquisition. What he or she stands to gain.
- What the person stands to lose.
- Likelihood that the employee will stay with the company (including specific forces that would persuade the person to stay and how to increase these and thereby tie him or her to the firm if that is what is desired).
- Specific forces that would be an influence in leaving (including how to increase these or eliminate them, as appropriate).
- Problems/risks—or benefits—of the person leaving (include impact on other people, and how this might influence them to leave also; critical roles the individual plays in the organization's social system).
- Who, if anyone, should or could replace this person if he or she leaves.
- How well the person will adapt to the parent company's management philosophy and operating style.
- Key backers or advocates this person has in the firm. His or her adversaries in the acquired firm.
- Personal idiosyncrasies.
- Questions or concerns the owner or CEO has regarding this individual.

This key executive might be asked, in closing, for any additional conclusions or recommendations that would affect the disposition of the incumbent in the postmerger environment. Finally, it can be helpful to have this top executive in the acquired firm categorize each of the key subordinates on the following scale:

- Should be separated from the company.
- Questionable need to keep with the company.
- Not critical whether the employee leaves or remains.
- Efforts should be made to keep the employee with the company.
- Critically important to retain.

PROFESSIONAL EVALUATION BY A MANAGEMENT/ORGANIZATIONAL PSYCHOLOGIST

Step two in the three-pronged approach to evaluating key incumbents consists of an in-depth appraisal by an outside professional, someone who has the unique tools and also the objectivity needed to add an important dimension to this audit of the acquired human resources.

Ordinarily, the management/organizational psychologist will conduct a thorough background interview with each person as well as some additional paperwork and possibly testing. As part of the face-to-face inquiry, the psychologist should delve into such areas as the incumbent's career objectives and feelings regarding the merger. Specifically, the individual being evaluated should be given the opportunity to speak at some length about his or her feelings concerning the parent company, fears and concerns relative to the acquisition, etc.

This exercise is sometimes threatening to those who are asked to participate, and for that reason they probably should be assured that they will be given the opportunity for a "feedback session" with the psychologist responsible for gathering and interpreting the data. This second meeting is most likely to occur several days—maybe even a few weeks—hence, thus, it provides another chance for the person being evaluated to open up and freely ventilate feelings and opinions about the corporate marriage. Frequently this allows data to surface regarding how the merger is being perceived or how the parent company might take steps to overcome problems that are developing.

While the people who are asked to participate in the professional evaluation may be a little uneasy, somewhat wary about it all, they also are inclined to view it as a noteworthy effort on the part of the acquirer to deal with people in the purchased firm in an equitable, informed fashion. Most people will open up and talk much more freely with an outsider than with parent company executives, particularly if this third party displays a good grasp of merger dynamics. Almost always, the key people in the acquisition appreciate the opportunity to tell their story, to make a pitch for themselves. Furthermore, if arrangements are made for individual follow-up sessions to go over the data, participants may get a once-in-a-lifetime chance to hear a professional person advise them in a supportive, insightful manner on matters such as:

- How strengths can be played to most effectively.
- How weaker points can be compensated for, maneuvered around, or perhaps overcome completely.
- What developmental steps could contribute most to career effectiveness.
- What changes the merger/acquisition may call for in terms of management style or work habits.
- What job opportunities it would be most appropriate to seek in the new corporate setup, and which ones would carry a high potential for failure.

Parent company executives, in turn, get a very quick and very thorough feel for what they have acquired in terms of managerial and technical resources in the acquired firm. Management succession planning can thus proceed more promptly, and in a far more sophisticated, strategic fashion. The professional evaluation eliminates the need for much guesswork as the new owner goes about making staffing decisions. Moreover, in the months that follow, there are far fewer unpleasant surprises that crop up because people in the acquired firm were initially misread, misunderstood, and miscast.

EVALUATION OF KEY PERSONNEL IN THE ACQUIRED FIRM BY COMPANY EXECUTIVES

Top management in the acquiring organization should be involved in the third aspect of the appraisal process. In this exercise, top management should meet with those responsible for carrying out the assessments in steps one and two. Here, in joint session, the objective is to pool insights, weigh the ramifications of the data, and draw final conclusions regarding the disposition of those personnel who are under review.

Parent company executives play a very key role in this stage of the three-way evaluation. Their responsibility is to critique the key people in the acquisition on a number of crucial factors—e.g., personal chemistry, technical skills, operating style, corporate culture, etc.

It may be, for example, that the top executive in the acquired firm gives particularly good marks to one of those directly reporting to him. Likewise, the management/organizational psychologist may submit data endorsing the idea that the person is, in fact, just as strong and capable as the superior indicated. But if senior management in the parent organization has experienced a personality conflict or "bad vibrations" in meeting and interacting with this particular person, there may be little hope of a compatible working relationship. It could also be, however, that the other two data inputs, plus the facilitative influence of the management/organizational psychologist, enhance the parent company's understanding of and respect for the individual in question. And instead of a highly promising person being terminated or allowed to bail out because of interpersonal friction with the new owner, a mutually rewarding relationship may be allowed to evolve.

It is when the inputs from all three stages of the evaluation converge that accurate, serviceable answers are found to the questions of "Who should go?" "Who will (and should) stay?" and "How can those people who do stay best be managed and motivated for the success of the merged organization?"

7

Making Mergers Motivate

Corporate marriages are rarely followed by honeymoons. Employees in the acquired organization, as well as those executives responsible for striking the deal, tell endless war stories of the problems, frustrations, and surprises that so commonly follow on the heels of a merger. Once the marriage has been consummated, there is little time for rejoicing or making merry. If there is a honeymoon, it is invariably short-lived. In the best of circumstances it is followed by a "little period of adjustment," but a big percentage of the time there is severe marital trauma, and it lasts much longer than necessary.

If there is any honeymoon, it probably did not occur by chance. It did not come about because management in the two firms sat back to enjoy the rosy glow of the new relationship. Rather, any honeymoon-like atmosphere that exists comes about through careful, deliberate, insightful efforts to do the following:

- Pick the right mate.
- Engage in an honest and meaningful courtship.
- Communicate effectively.
- Be flexible.
- Monitor the impact each is having on the other.
- Respect each other's differences (in terms of values, habits, needs, and idiosyncrasies).

Even with all of that effort and the best of intentions, marriages and mergers give rise to people problems, and these difficulties usually begin to surface rather rapidly after the ceremony.

Intense managerial focus is absolutely essential as the two parties to a merger/acquisition strive to come to grips with the changes that are inherent in the situation. It is an environment where certain changes cannot be avoided and other changes should be actively sought. The conditions that exist during this period are ideal for implementing certain things, but early merger blunders can abort the prospects for eventual financial success. Free-floating changes, for example, meaning those that occur without outside direction and guidance, frequently flow in a negative direction. Change that is not monitored and properly guided can quickly get out of hand. This is why so many "maintenance managers," those defenders of the status quo, ordinarily experience—even create—monumental difficulties in the merger/acquisition transition process.

POSTMERGER DRIFT

The difficulties companies have in managing the change process are manifested in tangible ways during the months and even years that follow the merger event. Almost always there is a lull, a loss of momentum in the acquired firm. Westinghouse acknowledges, "it is fair to say that the disruptive effect of a Westinghouse takeover is of longer duration and more intense than is generally believed."

Experience shows that in most mergers the greatest lull happens during the first few months. Companies then slowly revitalize, but often take a period of one-and-one-half to two years to fully recover. Some, of course, never do seem to be the same, although the initial intent probably was for the acquisition to represent some sort of synergistic hookup between the two organizations.

This phenomenon is comparable to the postoperative period of recuperation experienced by the patient who undergoes surgery. That person will show a drop-off in productivity, his or her morale will usually suffer until physical and emotional strength have been regained, and there will be difficulty mobilizing personal resources against the environment. Acquired companies usually struggle through a similar adjustment process.

The severity of the episode depends heavily on the nature of the takeover—whether it was fiercely resisted or jointly sought—but the results are almost always counterproductive so far as productivity, profitability, employee motivation, and morale are concerned. In fact, postmerger drift has become such a common occurrence that it is basically viewed as an inherent reality within the merger process, something that just goes with the territory. Acquirers seem to regard this symptom pattern as something that is expected and must be tolerated when you are in the merger business.

This view is far too pessimistic. Listlessness and sagging productivity are not a given, at least not to the extent that is commonly expected. The intensity and persistency of postmerger drift can be pared to a minimum. But to overcome this interlude, this perfor-mance sag, the parent company will almost always have to take a hands-on approach. Top executives must move decisively and purposefully—not simply to make changes, but to make the right changes and then intelligently manage the organizational dissonance that is created.

The company must not be permitted to gear down as the work force moves into a wait-and-see stance. If they are allowed to respond to their own instincts, people will usually move into a holding pattern. And depending on the parent company's reaction, the downward trend that develops usually bottoms out within a 6- to 12-month period. Then begins the gradual and often halting uptrend over the next two years. Eventually, corporate effectiveness should equal and hopefully surpass the premerger level. Sometimes, of course, it never does.

Also, the cost of the preceding slump can never be fully regained. Lost revenues and key employees cannot be recovered, and there are other intangible costs. Lost productivity is more easily identified and the dollar figure assigned, but management rarely puts a price tag on those opportunities that were not seized because of the malaise brought on by the merger. Likewise, it may take several years for corporate statistics to accurately reflect how postmerger drift enabled competition to gain an edge on the floundering firm.

Figure 7-1 charts the common pattern of organizational performance during the first two years following acquisition. Operating effectiveness is sabotaged by the psychological shock-waves and resulting reactions of employees. Most of the time the extent of the postmerger problems is not valid evidence that the parent company is deliberately disregarding the management and human resource concerns of the acquisition. Management cares, but so often makes the wrong moves. Just how much deterioration there is in operating effectiveness, and how long it lasts, is dependent on (1) what kind of acquisition scenario is involved and (2) how astute-ly the company is managed after the fact.

Figure 7-1 Postmerger recovery period

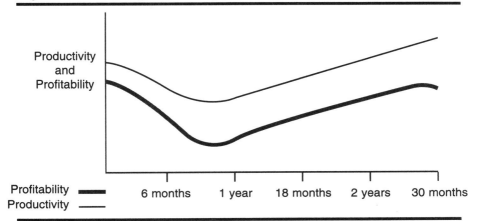

Productivity
and
Profitability

Profitability ━━━
Productivity ───

6 months   1 year   18 months   2 years   30 months

THE MOTIVATING POTENTIAL OF MERGERS AND ACQUISITIONS

Mergers invariably destabilize organizations and create dissonance. This upheaval, this disturbance, in turn becomes a motivating force as it causes people (and organizations) to strive for resolution or restabilization.

Now there is no question that the motivating influence is created. The issue that is up for grabs is whether the dissonance will be a constructive influence or a counterproductive one. If it is not understood, carefully monitored, and deftly managed, the dissonance will wreak havoc on a number of fronts.

Dissonance, in and of itself, is not bad at all. Without it people sometimes get into a rut and become complacent. Organizations do the same thing. When there is a high degree of contentment or satisfaction with its state of affairs, a company can be highly resistant to change. There is not enough introspection or enough challenging of the traditional way of doing things. Morale may or may not be high, but invariably the opportunities for operating improvements are not being seized and implemented. Usually people aren't being stretched. There is plenty of research to indicate that, unlike cows, contented organizations do not necessarily produce more, neither do they consistently produce better. Past a certain point, contentment becomes complacency, and the result is underutilized resources. There may be signs of creeping mediocrity as employees become habituated to living with the status quo.

Dissonance, the great motivator, develops when an organization encounters circumstances where traditional practices no longer seem to suffice or, at least, where people think they won't. Naturally, that is one of the things people worry about when their firm has been acquired, and that's one of the reasons the merger really gets their attention. Dissonance also occurs when there is a significant discrepancy between (1) what is perceived as the actual state and (2) the desired condition of an organization.

When a company grows stale and needs revitalizing, dissonance must somehow be created. Sometimes this can be accomplished by the impact of a strong individual who can function as a change agent. Mergers produce the same effect by being a change event.

In fact, when significant organizational change occurs, it is far more likely to result from some sort of impact coming from the outside rather than from pressures that develop within the firm. Mergers represent precisely this sort of external pressure point. The event of being acquired has an "unfreezing" effect on people's behavior, leaving them far more amenable to behavior change than they may have been at any other point throughout their careers. Managers as well as the rank and file suddenly feel a need to examine their performance, their contribution, their work style—perhaps for the first time in years. Some people will recognize new competition in the other organization. Likely a few employees will perceive some new and exciting horizons and view the merger as an opportunity for accelerated career advancement. Others, however, fear they will be adversely affected by the consolidation or integration of departments and functions.

Mergers bring about a reorienting process that operates in almost the same way as New Year's resolutions. More often than not, the merger will call for some kind of reorganizing and restructuring of one or both firms, so it represents a starting-over point. Mergers create new possibilities as well as new problems. Perhaps a merger is a chance to breathe fresh life into a financially ailing firm. It may be entry into a new technology or marketplace. Sometimes it means an introduction to a new operating style. Certainly the fresh ideas, new blood, and additional energies a merger brings can be key ingredients in the renewal of a sluggish company's vitality.

Ordinarily, mergers will greatly accelerate a firm's movement through the corporate life cycle. Mergers bring fast-paced change, and the resulting organizational shake-up can be a positive event for companies that have stagnated and not kept pace as they should. Moreover, even healthy companies can capitalize on merger dynamics when top management makes a conscious effort to use the merger for motivational purposes.

Ideally, mergers and acquisitions should be used for morale building, attitude improvement, innovation, and increased productivity. But without deliberate, strategic planning directed toward these goals, a company is likely to be motivated along negative lines as people experience fear, threat, and anxiety.

When top management in the parent company elects to keep its distance, to take a hands-off approach for an indefinite period of time, the dissonance simply is not managed and utilized in a constructive fashion. A remarkable opportunity is lost. There is a fairly narrow "time window" during which management must make its move, seizing upon the destabilization so that it can be turned to the organization's good. If people in the acquired firm are left to cope with the dissonance on their own, it is inevitable that some of them will adjust to the situation in a maladaptive fashion. When that happens, of course, the parent company loses the potential advantages of properly handled dissonance while inviting the troublesome aspects of dissonance that has been mismanaged.

Parent company executives should keep in mind that people in the acquired firm expect change. For them, in fact, simply being acquired has brought about a significant change, and they are mentally prepared for more to follow. They will even be anxious and uncomfortable if the acquirer, having finalized the deal, pulls back and assumes a passive stance. Granted, the incumbents don't want to be manhandled or overwhelmed with changes, but neither do they want to be ignored. They want to be attended to, preferably made to feel special. They want issues to be finalized or resolved, and don't like the feeling that they are merely in the eye of the storm.

In the merger/acquisition workshops that the author has conducted, there is an amazing degree of consistency in the complaints submitted by people in the acquired firm. The author's organization is regularly told:

- "We geared ourselves for change, and there hasn't been any."
- "We feel we're ignored; we're treading water."
- "You can't get an answer."
- "Company policies—what are they?"
- "There are too many contradictions when people from the parent company come here and speak to us; we get conflicting information."
- "They haven't given us anything to feel positive about."
- "We've lost the personal touch."
- 'There is too much uncertainty; we don't know which changes are coming."
- "We're suffering from a certain degree of stagnation, we're not going forward."
- "We've had a slowdown of progress."
- "We can't get answers to key questions."
- "Everything seems to be standing still; we hear good ideas, but we see no action."

So it's really a question of timing. The acquirer must walk a fine line between (1) imposing too many changes too fast and (2) letting the acquisition wallow in uncertainty and ambiguity.

There will be dissonance, though, and it is *not* necessarily something that should be eliminated as quickly as possible. If it is managed well—properly channeled—it can serve as a new energy force to fuel a valuable change process.

Regrettably, acquirers often make the mistake of trying to stifle the dissonance as quickly as possible. They want to calm people down and smooth things over. One of the tactics for accomplishing this is to keep a fairly low profile, offer reassurances that there are to be no significant changes, and largely do nothing vis-á-vis the target company for weeks or even months. As time goes on and the acquired firm becomes more and more habituated to the merged organizational framework, things do begin to restabilize and the dissonance begins to dissipate. Executives in the parent company will likely feel good about this and point to it as proof that their way of handling acquisitions works. Invariably, it hasn't worked nearly as well as surface appearances might suggest.

In the management vacuum created while the parent company follows a hands-off policy, the dissonance will have many negative ramifications—e.g., confusion, uncertainty, and weakening morale. Even though the acquired firm overcomes the initial organizational shock brought about by the change in ownership, that doesn't mean that it has made the adjustments that will sooner or later be necessary with regard to corporate culture, operating practices, management philosophies, and the like. The adjustment process that has occurred is, in fact, a superficial one. It merely glosses over differences for the time being and avoids dealing with changes that are ultimately unavoidable.

That's not good management. Even if in practice it seems to conform with what people in the acquired firm say about how they want to be treated, that's no proof that they really know what's best or that they will be happy with it in the final analysis.

What steps can the acquirer take, then, to capitalize on the dissonance, destabilization, and opportunities for change that exist? The remainder of this chapter focuses on several different steps or programs parent company executives can weave into an overall strategy for making the merger event a dynamic, constructive experience in corporate growth.

METHODS OF CORPORATE MOTIVATION

Involve Employees Through Surveys

Frequently the parent company is reluctant to engage in activities that go beyond making the necessary adjustments in accounting systems or personnel programs. They do not want to overburden either themselves or their new charges. At first glance this stance seems both logical and sensitive to the feelings of the people in the acquired firm. It gives rise to the comment, "Let's let the dust settle down a little before taking any action." Parent company executives may even add, "We want to give ourselves time to get to know the acquisition before we start making changes."

It all sounds so good. And it is true, time will have a settling effect on some situations. Other conditions, however, will only worsen with time.   And so often the parent company fails to take any really purposeful steps to achieve an in-depth, comprehensive understanding of the organization that has been purchased.

If the acquirer really wants to get a broad-gauged and unfiltered look at the company, there is logic in looking at it through the eyes of current employees. There will be differences in the perspectives of the various people—upper-level executives, middle managers, technical staff, rank-and-file workers, the field organization, etc.—but all points of view are important. Employees at all levels have attitudes and opinions they personally consider important, and they appreciate the opportunity to share their feelings, offer constructive ideas, or ventilate concerns.   Not only do they have information they are willing to share with the new owner, but the acquirer will also invariably find these insights to be extremely serviceable.

Probably the quickest, most efficient means for gaining access to all incumbents is to conduct an employee attitude/opinion survey. This is an excellent first step toward establishing direct communications with the employees, and it gets across two very important messages: (1) the new owner is genuinely interested in the firm that has been acquired, and (2) the new owner values what incumbents think and how they feel about their organization, the acquirer, and the merger in general.

The data that surface in the course of people filling out questionnaires and perhaps being interviewed may reflect bias, parochialism, prejudiced opinion, or distorted perceptions. But this is the database upon which employee behavior will be founded, regardless of how erroneous or illogical it might be. Much better for the parent company to understand the perceptions and attitudes at the outset as that at least makes it easier to manage in an informed fashion from the beginning.

A survey is a way for parent company executives to enlist the help of people in the acquired firm. It is a good step toward getting those employees to contribute to the new corporate cause. By participating in the generation of the database from which changes will emanate, employees share a greater feeling of ownership of these changes and are therefore more accepting of the changes and more committed to carrying them out in an effective fashion.   Instead of incurring employee resistance, top management defuses much of the opposition and replaces it with an involvement that is truly motivational.

A companywide employee survey in the acquired firm capitalizes on the human resources that come with the company. This is one of the richest, and most overlooked, sources for constructive information available to the acquirer.   Employees almost always know more than they are given credit for, yet they are commonly the last to be asked.   Employees can offer excellent ideas regarding better methods, new products, and existing or potential problems.   Ordinarily they will speak quite openly about interdepartmental frictions, the strengths and weaknesses of individual managers and supervisors, or operating tangles.   They will tell top management about changes that should come about subsequent to the merger, as well as which things are sacred and should not be tampered with.

It may be that a postmerger survey is the first time management has thought enough of employees to ask their opinions.   So the survey represents a golden opportunity for the new parent to become a hero.   Another neat feature of a survey is that the acquirer does not have to "own" the problems or gripes that surface in the course of data gathering.   Instead, parent company executives get to be the good guys who step forth to solve old problems.

Some executives might be reluctant to use the acquired firm's employees as a data source for fear of information overload.   But it is the surprises that do the damage, rather than too much information.   Not knowing what is happening out there in that cloud of dust does not take away the problems, neither does it eliminate negative attitudes or opinions.   Insufficient knowledge merely leaves one ill equipped to find solutions.   So the best time to conduct a survey generally is during the weeks that follow immediately on the heels of the merger or acquisition.   There is no better or quicker way for executives to get a global feel for the operation and to determine what has been inherited and which programs must be met.   It allows employees to work with, instead of against, the acquirer.   It motivates them through enlistment.   And it serves as a concrete demonstration of the acquirer's respect for the views of people in the acquired firm. Other benefits of an employee survey as a postacquisition management tool are:

1. Everyone gets a chance to have his or her say.
2. People can be as outspoken as they wish and still keep their face lost in the crowd.
3. A survey circumvents the normal communication channels in which information gets edited, lost, filtered, buried, or blurred before it reaches the top levels of an organization—especially in the merger/acquisition arena where communication problems abound anyway.
4. If done by outside experts, a survey brings objectivity and projects an image of equity.
5. From a systems viewpoint, a survey instrument can integrate the varying perspectives of people throughout the organization.
6. Finally, a survey provides baseline data that can be immensely helpful as management strives to track trend lines in attitudes and morale over time.

Make Some Tangible, High-Profile, Popular Decisions

An acquirer's first few actions vis-à-vis the target company are especially important. The first impressions formed will cast a long shadow; thus, it is crucial for the parent company to try and convey as positive an image as possible. Employees in the acquired firm will be extremely sensitive as to how they are being treated. They will be watching for even the most subtle signals that would give some indication of the personality of the parent firm as well as some insight into how they personally will probably be treated in the months ahead. Executives in the acquiring firm need to calculate their early moves in a strategic manner so as to motivate employees and get the merger/acquisition off to a favorable start.

It has already been pointed out that employees in the purchased firm expect changes and that within reasonable boundaries they want the parent company to come forth and make appropriate changes in a timely manner. Given this mindset of people in the acquisition, there are definite benefits that can be derived from the parent company moving promptly to do something for the good of the employees in the recent acquisition.

Top-level executives need to demonstrate that the new regime is action-oriented. Their first few interventions should be designed to illustrate the pace and direction the acquirer intends to maintain. The initial steps that are taken should communicate that the new organizational framework will not be a do-nothing, life-as-usual setup. And it should be emphasized here that the employees of the acquired company will draw their conclusions about the parent company by observing what it does, rather than what its senior executives say. In fact, there will be a great deal of skepticism regarding what is said or written by the acquirer, whereas anything that is actually done represents hard data. Therefore, the concrete evidence that begins to accumulate at the very outset of the merger needs to project favorable messages.

If possible, the acquirer should make some physical changes in the work environment that will be highly visible and which are certain to be well received by the work force. This may be something as simple as painting walls, adding some new pieces of furniture, or otherwise making physical improvements in facilities and equipment.

Another constructive step might be to set up various transition committees or task forces involving people from various levels, departments, or functional groups. The acquirer should take pains to see that the informal leaders and opinion makers are included in these merger projects, as these few people might have more impact on the entire organization than some of the senior executives do. It is important to get these influence leaders to work for rather than against the acquirer.

In any event, the parent company should do some positive and tangible things. It is particularly good timing to schedule these actions for immediately after the employee survey has been completed and analyzed and the results made known. This demonstrates to the employees that not only are they heard, but also that their input is taken seriously and that something is being done.

Utilize the "Pygmalion Effect" (the Self-Fulfilling Prophecy)

Put briefly, the Pygmalion Effect says that, to a large extent, we will get what we expect from other people. What we anticipate will tend to become a self-fulfilling prophecy as people begin to mold their behavior accordingly

One of the reasons for this phenomenon is that our expectations regarding others will influence the way we interact with them, causing us to reinforce certain aspects of their behaviors while ignoring or at least failing to reinforce others. Of course, all of us are victims of selective perception. We are prone to see those things we expect to see, while failing to observe other actions or events that are just as salient or perhaps even more significant.

Then, too, people seem to have a way of giving much the sort of behavior we let them know we expect from them. In a sense, whenever we communicate an expectation, we establish a goal or behavioral objective. Granted, some people may reject our expectations, and even take pleasure in behaving counter to what we would have anticipated from them, but it is uncanny how much of the time people will deliver what we expect.

In the merger/acquisition environment, then, parent company management should strive to motivate employees with new expectations. Executives should challenge the work force of the acquired company by setting fresh and somewhat higher standards of performance. This is a highly appropriate time to make people stretch.

As already mentioned, mergers and acquisitions cause people to examine their behavior and reevaluate their modus operandi. This introspection, plus the destabilizing effect of the merger/acquisition, causes them to be much more open to behavior change. Astute executives will seize this opportunity to call more of the employees' potential into play.

It is imperative, however, that any new and more demanding standards of performance be communicated clearly. And it is absolutely essential that parent company executives communicate their total confidence in people's ability to measure up. It is not enough to just notch up the bars so that the hurdles are higher. The work force must grasp the idea that the parent company believes in them and has no doubt about their ability to make the grade.

Most people upgrade their performance automatically when confronted with a leader who expects more of them and expresses confidence in their ability to measure up. What so frequently happens in the postmerger setting, though, is (1) expectations are not communicated clearly at all or (2) employees in the acquired firm somehow get the idea that the parent company views them as less capable or as possessing questionable ability to meet new performance standards. As a result, the Pygmalion Effect works in reverse. People in the acquired firm become less motivated and do, in fact, suffer a loss of confidence.

Generally speaking, employees would prefer to contend with higher performance requirements that are made clear rather than blurred, ill-defined standards that aren't particularly demanding. They just want to know how the measuring stick works and who will do the measuring. Finally, they respond favorably to high expectations when it seems that top management genuinely has faith in their ability to achieve at that level.

Provide a Sense of Corporate Direction

Just as people can be challenged to perform better when they are confronted with more demanding expectations, they also are motivated to upgrade performance when they are given a clear sense of direction. The acquirer who steps forth promptly to structure organizational goals for employees provides a crucial focus for organizational resources. Many of the conventional problems associated with mergers and acquisitions are a direct offshoot of people going off on tangents, operating in a fog, or essentially shifting into neutral for lack of well-defined goals.

Research has proved very convincingly that resources, whether individual or organizational, will gravitate toward clear goals. But employees in an acquired firm routinely are left to operate for months without any clearly defined targets. Parent company executives may intend for the acquisition to continue running on the same set of tracks in pursuit of the same corporate objectives. But incumbents frequently are not convinced that this is really the case even if the new owner says so. Employees are inclined to remain skeptical until it is obvious that the acquirer really understands what existing goals and objectives are and reaffirms these in writing.

Of course, all too often the acquired firm (or at least a certain part of it) has been operating without a set of specific, concrete, and measurable goals that are well integrated. Various departments or corporate functions may be working at cross-purposes, some parts of the company may be wandering aimlessly and still others may be charging ahead with a vengeance but actually going in the wrong direction. These situations seriously undermine organizational effectiveness and certainly indicate a need for the acquirer to intervene.

Newly merged or acquired organizations need road maps with well-charted routes and specific destinations. But it is very common for employees to muddle around for a year or more before they finally figure out what is going on and where the new company is headed. Often management has little more of an idea than the employees have and allows the merged/acquired company to drift, hoping all the while that it will resume its normal pace and that everything will come out well in the end. Unfortunately, evidence suggests that this is usually not the case.

Top management needs to move with great haste to get people focused on the future rather than allowing them to wallow in uncertainty or the nostalgia of "the way we were." Managers and employees alike need definite aiming points, something to shoot for, as without a good sense of purpose, inertia will creep in perniciously.

The difficulty in providing people with serviceable goals and operating objectives comes from the fact that things in one or even both organizations are often in a state of flux. Priorities need to be reassessed and resources reallocated. People in the management ranks have to agree on how the corporate thrust will be redirected. It can take quite a long time to go through these exercises properly and, meanwhile, postmerger drift can set in and represent a further drag on employee motivation.

What is most needed at this stage of the game is an intense focus on short-term targets. Long-term goal setting requires more time and effort, and there is more guesswork involved. Furthermore, people will benefit from seeing short-range goals achieved. It pumps them up, builds confidence, and restores momentum to the corporate machine. Some of the interim goals or short-term objectives should be related to the merger situation itself—that is, they should be transition goals that are designed to help facilitate the integration process.

In the process of framing these new goals and operating objectives, management should take great pains to see that the goals are well synchronized. It is easy for different people to come forth promoting different objectives that actually are in conflict so that individuals or groups end up working at odds. There is little value in having managers push hard for the attainment of their respective priorities when they end up in hot pursuit of incompatible objectives.

Of course, it's not enough just to set goals, or even to make sure that those goals which are identified are well synchronized. They also have to be communicated to the people who will be responsible for their achievement. This calls for a lot of publicity. Management needs to keep the spotlight on the targets that have been established, and also arrange for regular, frequent, and specific feedback regarding progress toward goal achievement.

Employee performance is greatly enhanced when people are given well-defined goals together with frequent readings regarding their performance and the progress they are making. In the postmerger environment, these elements so often are missing. The result is that people get mired down and preoccupied with the here and now instead of attacking the future in a vigorous, well-focused manner.

Take an Affirming Stance

For most people in an acquired firm the acquisition is a threatening experience. It creates feelings of uncertainty. In fact, when top management is simply taking some of the steps recommended here— e.g., communicating more demanding expectations or establishing a new corporate direction—employees are likely to grow more uneasy. The natural tendency is to also become more inhibited in work behavior. People grow more cautious and they are less willing to take reasonable risks that would actually benefit the organization.

Parent company personnel frequently foster such inhibited behavior and fuel employee concerns unintentionally. This happens when their manner or attitude toward people in the acquired firm is impatient, critical, or condescending. People at all levels in the acquisition will be hypersensitive, and their pride is easily injured. It takes very little provocation to put them on the defensive, make them more inhibited, or demotivate them.

Parent company executives should take pains to establish and maintain a congenial climate—that is, one that is encouraging, supportive, and positive. All of the people in the parent firm who will have direct contact with employees of the acquired firm should be given formal coaching and training on how to best enter the acquisition and how to interface with people there. Personnel from the parent firm should be instructed to take advantage of any opportunity to praise individuals and groups—publicly, privately, in writing, or in person. The new organizational climate should be affirming rather than critical, encouraging rather than threatening, challenging rather than inhibiting. Employees in the acquisition must be given a feeling of importance.

Many employees of the acquired firm will be frustrated with the feeling that they have to prove themselves anew to a cadre of unfamiliar executives. This frustration is further aggravated when the acquirer descends on the target firm like an invading army that has conquered and is sending in occupation troops. So it's a time for humility on the part of all representatives of the parent firm, as well as a time for ego-building efforts to be directed toward people in the acquisition.

Give People a Flag to Wave

If the new work force is to be integrated, truly merged, then this should be done promptly. People in the acquired firm need to be given a sense of citizenship in the new corporate structure. Demotivation rapidly sets in when top management in the parent firm chooses to straddle the fence, neither assimilating the work force nor letting it stand independently.

Companies suffer a loss of identity upon being acquired and with that loss there usually is an erosion of commitment. Motivation deteriorates as "the company" becomes a less well-defined entity to which people can maintain an emotional attachment. Furthermore, personal ties to upper-level managers or the owner may be severed as these people leave the scene, eliminating important personal loyalties that previously generated strong motivational forces.

Of course, there are some companies (Beatrice Foods is a good example) whose acquisitional philosophy has done little to threaten corporate identity. As Beatrice bought out such firms as Samsonite, Stiffel, La Choy, and Gebhardt, there undoubtedly were many employees who never really experienced any change in ownership. Beatrice made a deliberate effort to let acquisitions keep their individuality. Each subsidiary continued to use its own name and company colors. The less apparent it was that a merger had transpired, the better.

If the acquisition's old corporate identity is to be eliminated, though, the parent (or surviving) firm has an obligation to bring acquisition employees into the fold. They need to be given a sense of the parent company's history and indoctrinated with its values, norms, and corporate philosophy. Naturally this must be done in such a way that it does not offend. It should not be delivered as propaganda or look like an attempt to brainwash, but represent an honest and humble effort to communicate the new corporate culture and the role the newcomers will play.

Nail Down Roles, Responsibilities, and Working Relationships

Immediately after the deal has been consummated, all echelons of management in the acquired company need a redefinition of their authority, reporting relationships, and accountability. Additionally, they should be given a crystal-clear understanding of the standards of performance they will be expected to achieve.

These steps should be taken as quickly as possible after the consummation of the deal. If necessary, the acquirer should sacrifice detail for speed. The main thing is not to leave acquisition employees operating in a vacuum, or some will do nothing while others do wrong. Either way, they usually create secondary problems that then must be addressed. These are the causes of so many postmerger brush fires that distract top management from maintaining a major focus on corporate integration.

It is commonplace for an acquirer to assume that it has done a satisfactory job of communicating to people who's in charge, who reports to whom, and what's expected of everybody. But in the post-merger surveys the author has conducted, and the merger/acquisition workshops the author has run, people constantly complain about confusing lines of authority and an ill-defined power structure. Employees invariably feel as though they must operate in too much of a fog. The situation breeds frustration and tangled relationships, with the end result being still another blow to employee motivation. Acquirers should recognize that, until these issues have been sorted out, people really cannot complete the adjustment process and become fully reconciled to the merger/acquisition.

Conduct Team-Building Sessions

Whenever there is to be a true merger, an actual blending of organizations, conflicts and competitive struggles will develop. People will jockey for position, play organizational politics, and vie for scarce corporate resources. In fact, there is usually an undesirable amount of this sort of infighting even if being acquired leads to little more than a reorganization within the target firm. These internal battles divert attention (i.e., human resources) from more constructive pursuits, while also contributing to problems regarding employee morale and motivation.

The conflicts are understandable, quite predictable, and rather difficult to avoid. People want to protect and sometimes expand their own turf. There are personality differences to reconcile, discrepant modes of communicating that need to be synchronized, ingrained management practices that don't mesh, and disagreements over resource allocations and which objectives should be pursued. In the process, egos come into play and issues are emotionalized. Eventually, relationships become sufficiently strained and the persons involved lose enough objectivity that a skilled, nonpartisan third party needs to be called in to help all parties work through the problems. The process is called team building, and the third party is usually an in-house or external consultant specially trained to serve as a facilitator.

The team-building process is an intensive exercise designed to (1) help an organization overcome dysfunctional group and individual behaviors and (2) realize more of its inherent potential. Team building is a potent tool for:

- Helping people learn how to work together.
- Improving communications.
- Clarifying priorities and defining objectives.
- Working through interpersonal conflict.
- Overcoming role ambiguity.
- Identifying problem areas in team functioning.
- Building trust and mutual support.
- Providing the opportunity for a group to analyze its strengths, weaknesses, and overall performance.

Team-building efforts should involve upper-level executives and probably people from the middle-management ranks, as well. The intent is to overcome inter- or intracompany difficulties or blockages which interfere with the teams' competence or overall organizational functioning. Team-building sessions that are designed and conducted by top-notch professionals can greatly accelerate the formation of a cohesive management team, while also generating a remarkable increase in managerial motivation and company commitment.

Team-building activities should be seriously considered following any acquisition that was strongly resisted by incumbents. Also it is a relevant, constructive exercise when there is to be a high degree of integration of the two companies' work forces. The tactic of choosing to "leave people to work things out on their own" may represent noble intentions, but it usually is the wrong medicine. It amounts to leaving people to flounder and fight among themselves, struggling with their personal agendas instead of putting their energies fully to work for the company. Problems drag on for months, sometimes years, when a professionally conducted team-building project could have brought quick resolution and a new level of corporate momentum.

If the acquiring firm sees to it that the management/executive group is functioning as a team, and is well motivated, there probably will be little need to worry about the teamwork and motivation of lower-level employees.

PEOPLE MOTIVATION MAY MAKE THE DIFFERENCE

Before employees decide to support a merger, they must be able to answer satisfactorily for themselves, "What's in it for me?" And top-management's responsibility is to take definite steps that help the people come up with a favorable answer. Obviously, some employees will gain little, if anything. Usually some lose stature, and a few are likely to lose their jobs. Mergers do generate a variety of forces that tend to demoralize and demotivate. Therefore, anything that can be done to ease the transition and minimize the losses for all concerned deserves careful attention.

The positive aspect of all this is that the destabilizing effect of a merger creates a very good climate for change. Moreover, it is possible to prevent most people problems if top executives do their homework, then take informed, strategic steps to capitalize on the motivating potential a merger brings.

8

Guidelines for Merger/ Acquisition Management

The dynamics of mergers and acquisitions are such that many management headaches simply cannot be avoided. There are many problems that just go with the territory. Most of them, however, can be preempted and their effect minimized if the people in charge will only:

1. Take the right steps.
2. Take them quickly enough.
3. Prepare people mentally to live with the problems that inevitably remain.

People at all levels in the management hierarchy will not be able to prevent or solve as many problems as they would wish. But they can certainly create additional ones simply by not doing everything they should to be a facilitative influence.

Probably the biggest step one can take toward being an effective manager of mergers and acquisitions is to understand what a unique event they represent in the life cycle of an organization. As a method of corporate growth, they are revolutionary rather than evolutionary. And it is important to recognize that uncommon growth calls for uncommon solutions. For example, the executives, middle managers, first-line supervisors, and front-line employees who assume that their careers or the company will be well-served if they simply maintain their ingrained, traditional work styles will be in for a rude awakening. The merger/acquisition announcement heralds a time of change. It is a period that calls for management personnel to be agents of change and for rank-and-file workers to be receptive to change.

In this chapter, two different sets of guidelines are offered: one for the people in charge in the acquiring organization, and another for management in the acquisition.

GUIDELINES FOR MANAGERS AND EXECUTIVES IN THE ACQUIRING FIRM

1. Don't promise that things will remain the same in either company. Most people won't believe you anyhow, and most of those who do will later insist that you have lied or misrepresented things to them. Explain that there will be changes, but that extreme effort will be made to *(a)* consider the interests of each employee and *(b)* keep them as well informed as possible of forthcoming changes. Remember, if you acquire another organization and don't make some changes, the odds are 10 to 1 that you have failed to take advantage of outstanding opportunities to make various changes that would be constructive, are needed, and would be adapted to quite well by incumbents.

It is risky to be emphatic in proclaiming, "We plan no management changes," even when that is the truth. Likely as not, some employees will put you in the position of having to terminate them, and you will be accused of reneging on your promise.

A manager in a major southwestern utility company undergoing an internal merger (e.g., operating companies being reshaped and changed into divisions) submitted his own version of the three most common lies— "First, your check is in the mail. Second, I'm from the government, and I'm here to help you. Third, you will not be affected by the reorganization."

Nobody believes it except perhaps the people who say it. Employees want to have faith in the words, but deep down inside they skeptically take it as mere rhetoric, and they probably should.

2. Make few promises. In addition to the admonitions offered in the preceding guideline, you should realize that promises of any type, as a general rule, will end up making life harder for you. In fact, even when you communicate something through innuendo, you can create expectations that will later prove to be a problem. Your hints will often be taken as hard data.

3. Keep your promises. When you do go on record as making a commitment, be as good as your word. There is a tremendous need in the postmerger environment for you to instill confidence and concentrate on developing a high degree of credibility. Do everything you can to improve the trust level. Understand that target company employees' paranoia, guardedness, and suspicion are very natural reactions to the situation.

4. Do talk in specifics whenever you can. Try not to add to the ambiguity. Try to be structured in your approach. What seems obvious or dirt simple to you is often unfamiliar and complex to others. Explain things in clear, straightforward language—avoid in-house jargon—and don't be too sketchy or talk in too general terms. Always check for understanding.

5. Be acutely aware of the impact of your comments, even in routine conversation. People will be trying to read things into almost everything you say. An offhand remark or slip of the tongue and one of the best people in the target company could be gone. Discretion is critical.

6. Don't feed the rumor mill. Again, a casual remark or careless wording can crank up another rumor when you should be doing everything you can to short-circuit rumors, conjecture, and misinformation.

7. Provide more communication than usual during and after the merger/acquisition event. Strive to overcome the information vacuum that typically develops. Maintain closer than usual contact because everyone becomes increasingly hungry for information.

Ordinarily, mergers and acquisitions cause the communication channels to grow longer, as (a) more people are involved and (b) the distance from decision centers increases. Furthermore, information often begins to travel along different paths, and this makes it easy for some people to get left out of the loop inadvertently. Finally, people from the two firms may each have a different language or vernacular, so that more effort is needed to translate messages for them to be understood.

8. If you don't have the answer people in the acquired firm need, help them find it. Don't be responsible for giving them the runaround. Instead of being a buck passer, fill the role of problem solver.

9. In keeping with the preceding guideline, you should strive to go the extra mile. Be helpful. Look for opportunities to facilitate the merger process. Anticipate the needs, and the questions, of people in the other organization. Then take the initiative in meeting those needs. Get the idea across that you are on their side. This can help defuse adversarial relations.

10. Listen with the third ear. Pay attention to how something is said, as well as the actual verbal content of the message. The "process" by which someone in the acquired firm communicates may provide you with better information than do the words themselves.

Be alert to implied meanings and hidden agenda. Deal with the total message—e.g., what's not said as well as what is, the nonverbal as well as the verbal, what's implied as well as what's actually verbalized.

11. Be humble. Go out of your way to avoid behaving in a manner that might be construed as arrogance, feelings of superiority, criticalness, abrasiveness, etc. People in the acquired firm will be defensive. Don't threaten or intimidate, even accidentally, as there is enough anxiety out there already. Be respectful.

12. Overall, exercise your best public relations skills. Make people in the acquired firm feel important. Help make them feel like they are a welcome part of the corporate family, not a stepchild or adopted second-class citizen. Show empathy and patience. Be personal and try to have a human touch.

Try to get to know those in the acquired firm as people with names and certain jobs. Be encouraging, supportive, and generous with positive reinforcement. Show interest and concern. Don't ignore them or be indifferent, as that represents just one more blow to the individual and organizational ego in the acquired firm.

13. Be prompt. Act expeditiously. Even if you make a concerted effort to be timely, the acquired firm is almost certain to feel that things are proceeding too sluggishly, that it is taking too long to make decisions and take action.

Mergers and acquisitions mean that, in conducting business, things have to go through more channels. Decision making will be more blurred. Procedures will be changing and therefore more confusing. Do everything conceivable to tighten the response time.

14. Provide a clear sense of direction. Be purposeful. Any acquisition is more likely to be responsive to new leadership if there is straightforward communication regarding what the new leaders want done and how the acquired organization is expected to work toward those goals.

Respect the fact that uncertainty at the top increases the resistance to change at the lower levels. The acquired work force and management team are far more likely to rally and do battle for a new administration's goals if that leadership sounds the charge in an unambiguous fashion.

15. Establish—and   communicate—short-term   goals   and objectives. Keep people in the acquired firm focused and future-oriented. Make the targets specific, measurable, realistic, and yet challenging. Set definite timetables and deadlines. In the absence of goals that can provide a good sense of direction, the work force often shifts into neutral and begins to drift or coast.

16. As Antony Jay wrote in *Management and Machiavelli,* you should do one of two things: embrace the people and make them yours, or terminate them and get them out as quickly as possible. Get the surgery done with, then get on with business. Don't cut here, slice there, and after a while saw another limb off. Let the bleeding be done with so the healing can commence.

17. Don't just assume the acquired company will follow the parent company rules, policies, and procedures without being told what they are. In fact, employees of the acquired company probably will have to be told a number of times before the message takes hold as it should.

18. Guard against a common mistake in underestimating the time and planning required to appropriately manage the change process associated with mergers and acquisitions. Experience shows that small acquisitions often call for just as much attention and sometimes more hand-holding and getting-adjusted time than the large ones.

19. Establish clear, well-defined reporting relationships and lines of authority. Historically, the most unsuccessful mergers and acquisitions have suffered from unclear relationships and a tendency to change already vague, poorly defined reporting relationships several times in the first year.

20. Coach the parent company managers you plan to "send across" into the acquisition regarding how you want them to make their entrance or debut. This deserves a day of careful training involving discussion of the situation, consideration of cultural difference, plus an analysis of personalities and the management style people are accustomed to in the acquired firm.

21. Resist any inclination to fight back at employees in the acquired firm. Expect resentment, hostility, and criticism. Absorb it and talk beyond it when you deal with these people.

22. Don't relax once the merger/acquisition legalities have been consummated. Now comes the critical period of making the deal work.

23. Make a concerted effort to minimize corporate staff interference, especially by middle management personnel from the parent organization. Don't blitz the acquired firm with people who go in unannounced or unexplained.

24. Demonstrate a high regard for the limits of all available resources when establishing goals and timetables for the acquired firm. Objectives should be challenging but not unrealistic. You should strive to engineer success experiences rather than structure goals that are likely to be an exercise in frustration and futility.

It is critically important for your first few actions vis-á-vis the acquisition to be positive and successfully carried out. These first steps set the tone for the relationship and have far-reaching ramifications.

25. Be wary of replacing successful methods and procedures in the acquisition with new corporate rules from the parent company.

26. Guard against overwhelming the acquired company with paperwork, new reporting requirements, etc. Get people in the acquisition to help determine which existing reports and paperwork chores can be eliminated or perhaps allowed to remain in lieu of parent company requirements.

27. Realize you can't keep everybody happy. Unless parent company executives and managers play their parts right in the merger scenario, it is almost inconceivable that management in the acquired firm will handle things appropriately. As much as anything, the leadership in the target firm needs specific coaching regarding how the new owner expects them to perform in the postmerger setting. So much of the time, however, they don't get any guidelines that would give meaningful direction to their efforts to deal with the situation. So they play it by ear, make a multitude of mistakes, are condemned either overtly or covertly, and feel extremely victimized by the whole process.

The following section represents the sort of constructive guidance parent company executives should give to the management corps in the acquisition regarding how to deal with this sort of organizational event.

GUIDELINES FOR MANAGERS AND EXECUTIVES IN THE ACQUIRED ORGANIZATION

There is, quite naturally, generous overlap between the actions that should be taken by this group and by the parent company management team. Nevertheless, those items will be reiterated here in the form of instructions to incumbent managers in the acquisition.

1. Expect change. Prepare for it. Instead of fighting or resisting, embrace it. Posture yourself as a change agent or as a facilitator at least.

Certainly don't let yourself be surprised by the changes you will see or that you are expected to implement. Look toward the future, rather than futilely grasping the past and the old way of doing things.

2. Anticipate. Demonstrate a new level of initiative and resourcefulness. Look for ways to contribute to the integration process. The organization, and particularly your people, need more from you now than they have in routine times.

3. Stay goal directed. See that you operate with a sense of purpose, rather than moving into a holding pattern. Operate with clear-cut, specific objectives, even if they have to be very short range. Establish interim goals relative to the merger process itself.

4. Provide subordinates more in terms of management direction. Don't let your part of the organization fall victim to postmerger drift.

Employ a more structured management style. Give marching orders to your employees in a thorough fashion, including clear objectives with definite timetables.

5. Become a role model for a positive attitude toward the merger. Guard against being an insurgent, one who implicitly legitimizes a negative attitude toward the merger.

Look at it this way—if you didn't leave, you decided to stay. Make the best of it. Subordinates will be very sensitive to your attitude, however subtle the signals are that you send out. In the end, negativism (whether yours or theirs) is almost certain to make your job as a manager more difficult from a morale and/or productivity standpoint. Bad-mouthing the merger has very little promise of benefiting you, and it can be hazardous to your career.

6. Put more into your communication efforts. Invite input from subordinates and listen better. Then read between the lines.

Consider the need for more frequent meetings with subordinates to provide more opportunity for two-way communication.

7. Demonstrate maximum openness and candor (exercising prudence and the necessary discretion, of course). But don't feed the rumor mill with speculation, conjecture, or the repeating of damaging hearsay

8. Guard against making extremist statements or taking unnecessary stands vis-á-vis the merger. You may have to eat your words, swallow your pride, and end up with a lot of unnecessary heartburn. This is a quick way to lose stature and credibility in the organization.

9. Make few promises, even though people will be pressing you for hard-and-fast answers. Be wary of making commitments you may be unable to keep.

10. Be sensitive to shifts in the power structure. It is likely that the merger will result in changes in the way things get done or in the way decisions are made. Roll with the flow. Make the appropriate adjustments. Don't fight city hall.

11. Motivate to the hilt. Mergers destabilize and create dissonance in an organization. They serve as an unfreezing event, and this sort of organizational shake-up gets people's attention. It rattles their cages, making them introspect, evaluate their performance or worth, and consider the need for behavior change. The time is right to push for new and better behavior/performance. Capitalize on the motivating potential the merger creates. It is a tremendous opportunity to re–energize people and organizations that have grown complacent and perhaps a bit stale.

There is another point to be made here—if you don't seize the opportunity and use the dissonance as a motivator, it inevitably will be a demotivator for many people.

12. Expect slower response times. Usually procedures are in a state of flux. Policies are changing. More people, and new people, are involved in the decision-making process. Often there is a lack of clarity regarding just exactly who should be included in problem solving and decision-making activities. Keep in mind the fact that information flow has to cover greater distances and involve more people than before. Be patient.

13. Make the acquisition a two-way street. Get to know the other firm better. Learn how they do business. Make an effort to understand the parent company's values and management philosophy Get a clear fix on their goals for your organization. In short, get on their wavelength.

14. Remain a leader and decision maker. Don't let preoccupation with playing it safe cause you to abdicate.

Instead of letting all the confusion cause you to drift to the sidelines, wield your authority. You probably need to manage more, not less. And since mergers typically do slow response times, be sure you put forth more effort to be timely, decisive, and expeditious. Don't contribute to the slippage or loss of organization momentum.

15. Show some ownership of organization problems. Don't just project blame elsewhere and expect higher management (in your company or the new parent firm) to assume all the responsibility for collecting things. Instead of being a critic and finger pointer, strive to be part of the solution.

16. Help minimize surprises. It is the unanticipated event that generates the most personal stress for people. Be a therapeutic agent during these difficult times, instead of doing things that would add to the anxiety, trauma, and mistrust.

CONCLUSION

It is worth noting here that, in both the parent company and the acquired firm, the greatest sins of postmerger management are sins of omission. In opting to do nothing in an effort to avoid doing wrong, critical mistakes are made. It is, in fact, a time for stepping forth in a proactive fashion to take charge of the situation. There are opportunities to be seized and problems that should be attacked aggressively.

It is common practice for top management in the parent company to minimize the problems that develop in the acquiring and merging of another organization. Parent company executives generally give themselves pretty good marks for the way they have handled an acquisition. In strong contrast, people in the acquired firm commonly deliver scathing indictments of the way they have been treated. It seems that practically everyone who has lived through the experience of being merged or acquired has negative feelings about it.

At any rate, whether you listen to the people who have been there or whether you study the hard statistics, it is evident that management makes many mistakes in the merger/acquisition arena. It is treacherous terrain.

The truth of the matter is that companies not being merged or acquired are mismanaged all the time, too. But employees of those firms seem to get used to it. They become inured to the aggravations and frustrations that go with the status quo. Incumbents learn how to cope—they tolerate problems, learn how to work around them, and sometimes become a part of them. They resign themselves to the situation and learn how to survive in that environment.

But mergers and acquisitions bring abrupt changes, and people take notice of what's happening. The change in ownership gets their attention, breaks them out of their mental ruts, and generates concern and consternation. Organizational and individual inertia cause them to resist the changes mergers and acquisitions bring, and that will always be so. But let us hope that the record of management success in mergers and acquisitions improves, as there is much at stake for everyone involved.

Index

H

Heublein, Inc., 9-10
Heublein/Kentucky Fried
Chicken, 10
Hogue, James, and *Sun-Times*
acquisition, 28
Honeymoon and mergers, 96-97
Houston Oil and Minerals
Corporation and acquisition by
Tenneco, 15

I

Incline of resistance to acquisition, 32-33
Insurgents and obstructionists
among acquired management,
58-59
Intangible assets and cleaning
house, 82
Integrated planning and management challenge, 13
ITT, 8-9, 11
and O.M. Scott & Sons, 11

J

Jay, Antony, on management
retention and termination, 124
Johns-Manville Corporation, 9-11
and Holophane, 11

K-L

Kentucky Fried Chicken, 10
La Choy and acquisition by
Beatrice, 113
Leighton, Charles M. and
G. Robert Tod on questions
concerning acquired manage-
ment, 54-55
LTV Corporation, and raid on
Grumman Aircraft, 29-30

ORDER FORM
After the Merger:
Managing the Shockwaves

1-19 copies   _____ copies at $19.95 each
20 or more copies   _____ copies at $15.95 each

To place orders, call toll–free 800-992-5922,
or drop your order in the mail using this form.
Orders may be faxed to 214-789-7900

Name _____

Job Title _____

Organization _____

Phone _____

Street Address _____

P. O. Box _____

City, State _____

Country _____

Purchase order number (if applicable) _____

Applicable sales tax, shipping, and handling charges will be added. Prices subject to change.

Orders less than $100 require prepayment. $100 or more may be invoiced.

☐ Check Enclosed   ☐ Please Invoice

☐ **VISA**   ☐ **MasterCard**   ☐ **AMERICAN EXPRESS**

Account Number_____ Expiration Date_____

Signature _____

800-992-5922
Overnight or Second Day Deliveries
Available

96020

PRITCHETT & ASSOCIATES, INC.
13155 Noel Road, Suite 1600, Dallas, Texas 75240
214-789-7999 • FAX 214-789-7900

*Training programs also available. Please call 1-800-622-8989 for more information.

Call 214-789-7999 for information regarding international rights and foreign translations.

Management Consulting Services

Pritchett & Associates developed its in-depth expertise by working with *Fortune 500* clients for over 20 years. The key to our success is an intimate understanding of organizations undergoing major change. We combine extensive, "hands-on" executive experience with an analytic, results-oriented approach to problem solving. Our consultants have the know-how to:

- Exploit instability rather than merely cope with change
- Assess your culture, organization, and management processes to develop high-impact change initiatives
- Move you from plans to accomplishments...to become an adaptive organization
- Apply leading edge change management expertise and merger integration services to your critical business challenges.

Training Programs to Implement Change

Pritchett training programs build on the hard-hitting principles in our best-selling handbooks. These quick-impact, concentrated programs deliver a no-nonsense message on how to deal with today's rapidly changing business environment. Our training helps your organization:

- Accept—not resist—the predictable dynamics of change
- Underline why every employee must become a change agent
- Get people to take personal responsibility for making change work
- Protect—and even improve—operating efficiency and productivity
- Learn to communicate change effectively
- Keep employees focused on the "high-priority" issues—your business and your customers
- Recognize and capitalize on the opportunities created by change.

Price Pritchett is Chairman and CEO of Pritchett & Associates, Inc., a Dallas-based firm specializing in merger integration strategy and organizational change. He has authored 19 books, and is recognized internationally as a leading authority on merger dynamics and change management. He holds a Ph.D. in psychology and has consulted to top executives in major corporations for two decades.